Ghost Stories
of California's
Gold Rush
Country and
Yosemite
National Park

Antonio R. Garcez

RED RABBIT PRESS
HANOVER, NEW MEXICO

Other titles by Antonio R. Garcez:

New Mexico Ghost Stories ISBN 0-9634029-9-4

Arizona Ghost Stories ISBN 0-9740988-0-9

American Indian Ghost Stories of the Southwest ISBN 0-9634029-7-8

ISBN Number 0-9634029-8-6

*The author may be contacted for public appearances
at the following address:*
Antonio R. Garcez • Red Rabbit Press
HC 71 Box 496
Hanover, NM 88041-0496

Authors Note:

Some of the names associated with the storytellers mentioned in this book
have been changed. This was done for the sole purpose of protecting these
individuals because of their personal need to disguise their identity.
Thus, any name used in the book that might be associated with anyone
known to the reader is simply coincidental.

All photos were taken by the author unless otherwise noted:

Peggy A. Mosley, "Humes High School photo of Elvis,"
Neal Peters Collection, page 136

Lassen Loomis Museum Assoc.,
"Chief Shavehead of the Hat Creek Nation," page 150

Ralph H. Anderson, Chief Lemee, two photos, page 177

Bob Basura, Supervising State Park Ranger for photo permission re:
Sutter's Fort State Park, page 143

Craig A. Mattson, State Park Superintendent II/
Chief Ranger for photo permission re: Columbia State Park, page 97

Cover & book design and typography by
Kathleen Sparkes, White Hart Design
Editing by Kate Willis

Praises for
GHOST STORIES OF ARIZONA
by Antonio R. Garcez

"ARIZONA GHOST STORIES gives a hauntingly accurate overview to the many reports of haunted sites all over the state. It not only lists the places from north to south but quotes the interviews of eyewitnesses giving a remarkable feeling of being there with them as they encounter the unknown. Such sites as the Copper Queen Hotel in Bisbee to the Jerome Inn come to life in Mr. Garcez's investigations. His chapter on the reports of ghosts at Tombstone is perhaps one of the best accounts I have seen on this subject."

—Richard Senate

"The accounts range from sweetly sentimental to truly terrifying, but all share the benefit of Antonio's sensitivity and attention to detail. He shows respect for the tales, and those who tell them, and understands that history and culture are inextricably bound to all folklore."

—Jo-Anne Christensen

"Arizona could not have asked for a better chronicler of its supernatural landscape than Antonio R. Garcez. From Arivaca to Yuma, Arizona's most haunted places are all here! These stories will send shivers up your spine, and rightly so—they all really took place! If you ever wanted to experience something paranormal, let this book be your guide!"

—Dennis William Hauck

"These are not long-ago cowboy yarns, but very real, very current ghost stories from a rich and chilling mix of voices. Antonio has a rare talent for telling detail; he paints unforgettably creepy images that linger long after the book is done."

—Chris Woodyard

"The reader is transported into the world of the supernatural, by a great storyteller who weaves history and personal interviews into a series of riveting tales, sure to make your skin crawl! Here, restless spirits of the past meet present-day skeptics head on. Memories come to life in the stories from 19 diverse Arizona counties. The thoughtfully told, well-researched stories are sometimes frightening, oftentimes chilling, and always fascinating."

—Rob & Anne Wlodarski

Contents

Preface

To draw conclusions, to explain, or to define what is a ghost is not my role. Instead, what I sincerely wish to offer the reader with this book are stories of personal, paranormal events as they were narrated to me, face to face, accurate, without an overwhelming personal desire to embellish, or to "preen the feathers of self-esteem." These stories were presented to me within an interview format. My only "paranormal" tools were a pen, notepad, and tape recorder—that's all.

Whatever your own personal belief, or focus, I hope these stories will encourage you to "visit" with the persons interviewed, all of whom have experienced ghosts. There is much to be known, learned, gained, and in some cases, lost in making contact with the paranormal. I submit to you, the reader, that there is another existence beyond what we think is our only day-to-day "tangible" reality. There is no doubt in my mind that ghosts exist. None at all.

I am ever more grateful to the interviewees who have trusted this author enough to share and record their experiences. I hope that I have reproduced with genuine integrity their stories.

After more than a year of research involving visits to museums, sites of spiritual activity, cemeteries, and historical California landmarks, this collection of my most recent work does, with my own personal confidence, speak for itself. Even if you are a disbeliever of the existence of ghosts, these stories just might prove to be the "door" that "opens" your mind and leads you in another direction.

— *Antonio R. Garcez*

Acknowledgements

My deepest appreciation to my partner
Henry C. Estrada

Dedication

To Ishi, and all native peoples
within the historical area
of the state of California,
and to all the current
descendants of these most
cherished and beloved
ancestors, I honor your history
and exemplary culture.

It has been estimated that during the gold rush era, California's Native Americans numbered around 300,000. By the 1900 census only 15,000 remained. Unable to sustain themselves on their homelands, driven off, hunted as "wild animals," and decimated by foreign diseases, nearly 95 percent of California's Native American population had been wiped out. The gold rush and the subsequent invasion of white settlers into Native American homelands was for these historically peaceful and unique peoples nothing more than a policy of utter genocide. The historical record of events leading to a sustained effort by non-Native Americans to "remove the problem" of Native Americans living upon land rich in gold ore has been recorded, and is available to anyone willing to do the research and inform themselves. History is not always pleasant, but the facts cannot be denied in regards to the treatment of California's native inhabitants. This early, historical period was gruesome and undeniable. History, it seems, can be created and negotiated through context and perception. We must all take the responsibility to individually re-examine, and analyze historically, what we might believe to be "the truth." Re-examining the history of California's Native Americans is a good place to begin.

Death is not a period but a comma in the story of life.

Introduction

California! Yes, it's California the Golden State, known to many as a trendsetter, the land of plenty, the food basket of the nation, and the entertainment capital of the world. California, land of gold nuggets, palm trees, beaches, Franciscan missions, world-class wine, and diverse life. So much is offered by this uniquely beautiful state, that it would be pointless to condense its attributes here. What is central to this book is California's northern portion—gold rush country and Yosemite National Park.

Originally inhabited by various native peoples such as the Miwok, Chukchansi, Yokuts, Paiute, Mono, and many others, Northern California's native peoples were displaced and changed forever when the first influx of settlers came on the scene.

Obviously, this book's focus is the less talked about, but just as important, cultural basis of historical California—it's ghosts. You would be hard pressed to not find a resident of the gold rush area of Northern California who has not heard of, or had a personal brush with, on some level, the paranormal.

Within these pages are personal interviews with State Park rangers, store, hotel, and art gallery owners, an ex-prison officer, senior citizens, gay men, hotel front desk clerks, the curator of a Chinese temple, saloon owners, Native Americans, and many more. Frankly, I could not have asked for a more diverse and interesting cross section of individuals.

So, without further adieu, I present to you the ghosts of the California's Gold Rush Country and Yosemite National Park.

—*Antonio R. Garcez*

CALIFORNIA'S
GOLD RUSH COUNTRY
AND YOSEMITE
NATIONAL PARK

AMADOR CITY

Amador City and County are both named for the wealthy California rancher, Jose Maria Amador. The major creek he mined for gold was named after him, "Amador's Creek." Outcroppings of gold ore were numerous along Amador's Creek, which was extensively mined for the precious metal. In the summer of 1851, Amador City was established. Amador's first mines were the "Original" or "Little" to the north, and the "Spring Hill" located to the south, of town. The town's most productive mine was the "Keystone," which produced close to $24 million of the yellow ore.

Today, Amador County covers an area of 568 square miles of grassy, delicate rolling hills on its western edge and a craggy, rough mountainous landscape to its eastern boundary. The county was established in 1854, with the town of Jackson as its county seat.

In 1878, a devastating fire consumed almost every building on Amador's main street, sparing only two—the Fleehart and the facade of the Amador Hotel. As a result of the fire, new buildings were no longer built of wood but of brick and stone instead. Tin roofs also were incorporated into new buildings and attics were lined with sand and bricks in the hope of preventing dangerous, wayward sparks from taking hold. Safety measures such as these helped to preserve the majority of Amador's buildings for more than 120 years.

IVAN THOMAS'S STORY

I've lived in Amador all my life. My parents were both raised in Stockton, California. In 1924 they got married and moved to Amador City. Father was soon offered a better paying job with the state forest service at Lake Tahoe, and once again, they moved. In less than one year, father was injured on the job when a large tree limb fell and broke his right leg and hip. He was disabled from that day forward. With what little money my parents had saved, and with the money from my father's disability check, they moved south and purchased a small ranch house on 10 acres just outside of Amador City. A few months later, I was born. My birth was followed by my sister, Sandra, and my youngest sister, Helen. Today, out of all my family, the only ones left living are Sandra and myself. Sandra currently lives in a rest home in Sacramento. Sandra lived at the ranch house until she had to be moved to Sacramento. I couldn't take care of her, so it was decided the best thing was for her to move to Sacramento. Her son lives in Sacramento and is now able to visit with her more often. I don't think she'll live much longer. The last time I visited her, she didn't recognize me. So now it's just me and my small dog, Colonel. I raised Colonel since he was a puppy. His mother was kicked by a neighbor's horse, and the litter of puppies was left without a mother. I bottle fed this little guy for about a month before he could eat on his own. He's my little boy. He lets me know when anyone comes on to the property—living or dead!About three years ago, before Sandra moved away, Colonel was asleep out on the front porch. That's where I have his bed. You can go see it. It's right over there, under the bench. As a puppy he took to liking that cardboard box so much, that even after he got older, he would walk inside it and fall asleep. He's never been happier. I guess it makes the little guy feel safe. Well, one afternoon, while my sister and I were sitting at the kitchen table, we heard Colonel barking in the front yard. We walked outside on the porch and saw him barking and barking at nothing in particular. He just was barking at the thin air. I turned to my sister Sandra and asked her, "What's going on here?" We didn't have any explanation for our dog's weird behavior. Colonel kept barking, then suddenly we saw that the hair on his back began to rise, and he started to growl and make a low

"throaty" sound. We could see that his eyes were focused on an invisible "thing" and he was not about to change his gaze. Suddenly, he ran back as if something had lunged at him, then he quickly ran forward and tried to snap at whatever it was that had attacked him. This went on for a short time before we saw him recoil in pain, as if he had been hit with a stick, or kicked hard. I had had enough, and decided to intervene by placing myself between my dog and whatever it was attacking him. As soon as I had positioned myself in front of the dog, whatever it was made its way around me and into the house with Colonel bolting right behind! My sister and me were both caught off guard, and as Sandra stood holding the front door open with one hand, she made the sign of the cross over her chest with the other. My skin began to crawl.

My sister and I went into the house and found Colonel barking madly at one corner of the living room. It appeared as if the ghost was in the wall. Our dog was going nuts. In just a few seconds, Colonel stopped barking and he wanted to be let outside. When I turned him loose, he went straight for his water bowl and drank.

That day left both of us with many unanswered questions. Luckily, we both felt comforted by our dog's protective nature. We knew that if there were any future "visits" by a ghost, Colonel would not let them get the upper hand. Or so we thought.

A friend of Sandra's came over that evening and took both Sandra and Colonel to her home for the weekend. I decided not to let my fear get the better of me, so I chose not to leave.

Later that night I was awakened by a loud noise in the kitchen that sounded like a dish crashing to the floor. It startled me to the point where I stood sitting upright in bed! I listened for a few minutes and heard nothing more. Thinking I was dreaming, I decided to lie back down and try to sleep.

As I began to close my eyes, I heard the sound of a mumbling voice. A coldness came over me because I immediately knew the ghost had returned. I kept quiet, and could only make out that it was a male voice, but the words were not at all clear. There was also a tone of anger in the voice. A rapid muttering, mixed with anger, is how I would put it. So much was racing through my mind at that moment. I found it difficult to move. I decided to just lie in bed and hoped it would go away. Abruptly the voice stopped.

I didn't have to breathe a sigh of relief because something else soon started up. I began to hear the sound of footsteps

"I heard the doorknob begin to slowly turn."

coming down the hall from the kitchen, and they were making their way towards my room! I was completely and fully awake at that moment. I'm not ashamed to admit that I was scared.

As the footsteps came closer, I braced myself for what I might see. My imagination went wild with the thought of seeing a bloody face, a skull, or even something worst. As I said, my imagination was going crazy. As the footsteps reached my closed bedroom door, I heard the doorknob begin to turn slowly. I couldn't take any more. I jumped out of bed and turned on the lights. I grabbed the doorknob and swung the door open. There was no ghost, or anything visible at all. I was relieved, but also unnerved by the experience.

The next morning I phoned Sandra and described what I had experienced. She said that because of what we had both experienced with our dog the day before, the thing must have returned. I didn't want to allow my imagination to take the better of me. So I decided not to talk or think about it any further.

Later that same night, at around the same time as before, I was awakened by a dish breaking in the kitchen, and the footsteps started up again. This time, I knew I was not imagining any of this. This was real, and it was in my house!

I was even more scared than the night before. As the footsteps came closer and closer toward my bedroom door, I began to pray out loud. As the footsteps stopped outside my door, once again I heard the doorknob begin to turn. I kept quiet and opened my eyes wide. Keeping still, the door slowly opened and the sound of the footsteps walked into my room. I was shaking by that point, frozen with fear. I tried hard not to make any sudden move, and pretended I was asleep.

The footsteps came to my side of the bed and stopped. In a few seconds, I felt the side of my mattress compress as if someone had sat on it. No kidding, I actually felt the side of the bed move. At that moment, the word "fear" cannot begin to describe how I felt. Not knowing what to expect next, I felt the presence of a cold face brush against mine. I knew it was a face because I could hear its heavy breathing right in my ear! I was shaking.

The next thing that the ghost did was to laugh directly in my ear! It was a menacing laughter, a devilish and very evil kind of laugh. It wasn't very loud, but it was eerie all right. Something stirred in me right at that moment. I called the name of Jesus to help me as I sat upright in bed. Directly at the foot of my bed I saw the ghost! He was a short, round man, wearing a brown, French beret, a white shirt buttoned to the neck, and a brown suit. No tie or jewelry. With both hands he held on to the belt at his side as he glared at me.

Strangely, my fear subsided and I got the courage to speak "Why are you here?" He looked at me with an inquisitive face, and slowly bent over toward me. He paused, and then quickly leaned back and without making any noise, visibly let out a huge laugh! What ever he must have made of my question, gave him a lot of humor. He closed his eyes, and opened his mouth as he laughed and laughed.

I couldn't take my eyes off him. This whole experience took place in under a minute, definitely not any longer. Then this short, fat ghost began to disappear. Just slowly into nothingness. He laughed himself into thin air. I began to see the bedroom wall behind him as he started to vanish, until he had totally left the room!

I was left with a feeling of freedom. I knew that he would not be returning ever again. I somehow knew there would never be anymore footsteps, breaking glass, and teasing of my dog. He was gone for good.

Why was he visiting our house? Did he have a message to deliver? Who knows? Perhaps he didn't want to do anything more than have some fun before moving on to who knows where? Nothing paranormal has taken place in this house since that time. Nothing at all. I can't explain why this man would want to be in our house.

It's strange to admit, but I'm glad it happened to me. It scared the "you know what" out of me, but I'm better for the experience. Now I know for sure that this life is not the end of us. We go on further after we die to somewhere else, and I know that's for sure.

ANGELS CAMP

Aside from Los Angeles, there exists another "City of Angels" in California; this other city is better known as Angels Camp. Similar to other gold-rush towns of its time, Angels Camp had its boon, which ultimately went bust, and is now doing quite well in its revival.

History notes that a shopkeeper from Rhode Island, named Henry Angel, established a trading post for the miners in 1848. Apparently, Mr. Angel was not interested in the backbreaking work of digging for gold, but instead chose the less effortless manner of making a living by selling retail goods to the 4,000 or so miners.

In 1855 a devastating fire consumed many of the downtown wooden buildings in Angels Camp. The resilient town's folk commenced to rebuild the new structures out of fire-resistant stone and metal. These buildings also had their roofs insulated with dirt and sand, providing further protection from future fires.

Frequently visited sites in Angels Camp—aside from the quaint antique shops and museums lining downtown—are Mercer, California and Moaning Caverns, Greenhorn Creek golf course, and New Mellones Lake.

Mark Twain

Today the population of Angel's Camp is roughly 3,000. During special town events this figure swells substantially. One major event is the "Jumping Frog" contest, which takes place in May—Calaveras County Fair and Jumping Frog Jubilee. The town's historical resident, Mark Twain, in his story, "Celebrated Jumping Frog of Calaveras," made this contest famous. Today, a statue of Mark Twain is located in Angels Camp's Utica Park, paying homage to the well-known writer.

Mark Twain made Angels Camp and Calaveras County famous worldwide when he wrote of the "Celebrated Jumping Frog" in 1865. The author Samuel Langhorne Clemens, who was better known by his pen name, Mark Twain, left his historical mark on Angels Camp. Twain is recognized as a great American writer who transformed American literature into something uniquely American through his original use of language, setting, and colorful characters.

PHYLLIS MACCARIO'S STORY

I've worked here at Orphan Annie's Emporium for five years. Historically, the actual building where the store is located used to be a meat market. Before beginning work at the store, no one ever mentioned to me about any ghostly activities that were associated with it. However, the owner of the building that shares a common thick, stone wall with ours

told me, that many years ago, a man died in this building. After that brief conversation with the next door neighbor, I began to notice strange little unexplainable things. No one ever hinted to me about ghost activity at the store. But, like I said, strange, unexplained things started to take place just a few weeks after I started working there. I've seen darting shadows, and the shadows of someone walking around the store.

I do remember one time, after I had locked up for the day. I was by myself in the store, when an automatic sensor went off. The owner had placed a motion detector that is in the shape of a green frog, on one of the shelves. You've probably seen this very popular and common frog sensor for sale in department stores. A motion sensor is located in the mouth of the frog, which lets out a loud croak when it senses movement passing in front of it. This frog sits upon a shelf in the back of the store. Customers are at first startled, then they have a good laugh at it as they unsuspectingly pass in front of it, and it lets out a big *ribbit, ribbit!*

When I was alone one evening in the store, closing the register and counting the daily money, I heard the frog croak. I

"I heard the frog croak again, and again."

was startled by the sound, and froze in place. I waited a while, expecting to hear the footsteps of someone walking about the store. I looked around the tall display cases trying to see if I could spot someone hiding in the back of the store. The shelves are arranged in a manner that allows me to view directly between all the aisles of the store, so it's not at all difficult to see clearly without obstructions. As I moved my gaze about the store, I saw no one. Comforted by knowing that no one was in the store with me, I began to feel at ease. Suddenly, I heard the frog croak again, and again! That did it. I decided this was enough, and I stopped what I was doing, left the money in the register, and made for the front door!

During another evening as I was closing the register for the day, just like the first incident, an even stranger thing happened. I heard movement in the back of the store; the noise of someone tossing paper. Again, this was something new for me. I wasn't familiar with this strange noise, and again, as before, I wasted no time and made for the front door.

I recall an employee who had worked at the store for a short time, who told me that she would hear the sound of a man's heavily booted footsteps, going up and down the stairs. She would only hear these footsteps making noise in the rear of the store. The employee would always be alone in the store when the noises started. At other times, she mentioned that she would hear the voices of several people talking at the back of the store. Again, at the time of these incidents, no one but this employee would be in the store.

Not knowing what, or who this spirit is, we've decided to name the ghost "George." We named him George in order to make him seem more familiar and less of a stranger and threat. I do believe that this is the spirit that we've all had the encounters with. Now, we all get a little kick from talking about George, our resident ghost. Thankfully, he's never harmed us, and he tends to enjoy staying in the back of the store. Which is all right by me.

I've personally not only experienced the noises at the back of the store, but there have been other occasions when I've been standing at the front counter, and I've "felt"

"I've seen darting shadows."

someone watching me from the back of the store. It's as if there is a person standing against the back wall and his eyes are fixed on me. It's a very unnerving feeling. This feeling of eyes being focused on me has taken place many times. To this day I hesitate to look in the direction of the back wall unless absolutely necessary. I'm afraid of what I might see standing there. I don't know what I'd do if I saw George himself! You know, all this talk about what we've seen in the store is making me very nervous. I don't want to think about encouraging George to appear to me. Because I do spend a lot of time alone in the store, I think it's best not to talk anymore about ghosts.

SONORA

Sonora has been the center for county, government, and business since the mid-1800s. It is one of the most prominent towns in the Mother Lode, preserving its rich history while acting as the commercial hub for a three-county area.

St. James Episcopal Church, located at the corner of Washington and Snells Streets, dates from the 1850s. Better known as the Red Church, with its towering high steeple and very noticeable red color, it is one of Tuolumne County's most photographed buildings.

Many Washington Street business buildings date back to gold rush days, and a few of the businesses—including the Union Democrat—have been serving the public since the 1850s. The side streets have a number of Victorian-era homes built around the turn of the century for Sonora's elite. The Miwok Native American nation prospered in Sonora until the gold seekers came. Today's Washington Street is believed to follow a long-established Miwok trail. The Miwok welcomed and traded with the first onslaught of miners in 1848, but the Native Americans

were soon displaced as word spread around the world that the hills were rich with gold and more settlers moved in.

Miners from Sonora, Mexico, were the first to settle in what they called Sonorian Camp. Then came men from Canada, the Caribbean, China, the Eastern United States, Europe, South America, and the South Pacific. Traders followed and Sonora became the commercial center of the southern Mother Lode. The City of Sonora was incorporated into the county in 1851 and was named the county seat that same year. Life became quieter as easily-gotten gold disappeared, but even today Sonora remains the commercial and governmental center of the area.

Today, the city of Sonora's population hovers around the 5,000 mark. There is an additional "shadow" population of vacationers, shoppers, and downtown employees estimated at 12,000–20,000 people. One of the downtown historic sites that has been recently restored is the Opera Hall. In its previous lives the building was a stable, a garage, and a storage building. Today, the Opera Hall—which is a picture of its past—is the location for many community events, private parties, and art exhibits.

GERALD AND LEE'S STORY

I moved to Sonora about 15 years ago from San Francisco. Searching for a more peaceful and less stressful life, I had been contemplating making a move out of the city for several months. The daily grind of living in such a large city as San Francisco had become more and more of an effort. I wanted a stressless quality of life that I believed a smaller community like Sonora could offer.

Prior to my move, I was employed as a juvenile probation officer. My caseload of kids was between 38 to 45, a ridiculous number, and as much a stress-producing job as any could be.

In theory, I was supposed to make contact with each "client" once or twice a month, make contact with their parents, school, social worker, write reports that were submitted to the juvenile court, attend meetings, chart in the client's file, be called into court by deposition, and attend to numerous emergencies. The list went on and on. And all this was to be done

within a period of a month. I became psychologically numb, or as it is commonly termed within the department for a worker who has reached his limit, a "burn-out!"

So, 15 years ago I made the decision to leave my job, move, and settle into the more relaxed community of Sonora. I purchased a small, two-bedroom bungalow on the south side of town, a short walking distance to Main Street. I wasn't much into making new friends immediately. I wasn't antisocial, I just wanted to take things easy for a time and do some fixing up and gardening around the house. One of the renovations I made to my home was to turn a bedroom into a computer room. Soon after, I began my own designing and advertisement office–business out of this room.

Friends still living in San Francisco and my new acquaintances in Sonora began to use my skills and services. Quickly word got around about the new advertising guy in town, and within a week, I had acquired four accounts!

One of these new accounts was with a gentleman named Lee who, like myself, had moved away from a big city to seek the sanity of a smaller town. Again, like myself, Lee also had started a small, home-based business. Lee responded to the newspaper ad I had placed in the local paper, and when he stopped in to describe his advertising needs, we really hit it off. Unknowingly, our business relationship would become, in time, a great friendship, and eventually would develop into a romantic partnership.

At the time, Lee's business interest was in raising locally grown organic herbs and flowers. He singularly handled the full duties of the business from planting the seeds to harvesting to eventually distributing his organic produce to restaurants in the Sacramento area. Also, twice a week he would load up his Nissan pickup and attend the popular Farmer's Market in San Francisco. The town of Sonora also has a wonderful Farmer's Market located at its fairgrounds that Lee occasionally attends to this day.

Well, one day during one of Lee's initial visits to my home, as we were seated in my living room discussing the direction that he wished to go with his advertisements, he happened to mention an experience he had had a week ago. Lee began by

first telling me, "I know we don't know each other very well, so I hope you don't think I'm crazy, or some kind of a new-age loony, as I share this with you, but I've had an encounter with a ghost." I was of course taken aback by his announcement, but I assured him by stating, "I was a probation officer for several years. I can't imagine anything stranger than what I experienced on the job." After sensing my acceptance, Lee began the story of his encounter with a spirit. Little did I know at the time, but I would also share this "experience."

Lee began by telling me that one Friday morning, early, while on a produce run to Sacramento, he had decided to visit "Lillian," a 78-year-old female friend of his. Lillian, who lived alone on Sonora's north end, had recently been released from the hospital. She suffered from diabetic complications and a long battle with congestive heart disease. Lillian and Lee had become good friends over the years, and because of her ill health, Lee had become Lillian's transportation to and from her doctor and hospital visits.

The day before, on a Thursday, prior to driving to Sacramento, Lee had spoken to Lillian on the phone, and had told her he would be visiting her early the next morning. Lee said that she had sounded well and was in good spirits. The next morning, on a Friday, Lee drove up to Lillian's house, walked up to her front door and turned the knob. Finding that the door was locked, he gave a few loud knocks. There was no answer. Since Lillian did not respond to his knocks, Lee thought that Lillian must have forgotten about his visit, and had overslept. Normally, Lillian would have left the door unlocked for Lee. Lee told me that immediately he became concerned that something was not right. He called out her name, then heard Lillian softly answer, "Lee, oh Lee, come inside honey."

At this point in Lee's story, for some unknown reason, I became covered in goosebumps. I felt the hair on the back of my neck stand on end. Not wanting to interrupt his story, I kept these reactions to myself, and allowed Lee to continue.

Lee said he responded to Lillian's voice, saying "Lillian the door is locked. You need to unlock the door." When Lillian did not respond, Lee took a peek through the window and saw the living room was in darkness. Lee called out once again, "Lillian, unlock the door." Not getting a response, Lee walked to

"Lee took a peek through the window and saw a darkened living room."

Lillian's backyard, and up the few stairs leading to the porch door. He found the door unlocked and quickly entered.

Entering her living room, he could see that her bedroom door was open and the table lamp by her bed was on. Lee stood in the living room, and so as not to startle her, called out her name. When she did not answer, he cautiously walked into her bedroom where he found her lifeless body in bed. Lee said he reached to touch her round face, and when he held it in his hands, it was cold as ice! Lillian had no doubt been dead for several hours. Unable to hold back his tears, he said a few private prayers, then used her phone to notify the authorities.

I asked Lee the obvious question: "What he thought about Lillian's disembodied voice answering him from within the house?" He said, "I got a little scared—how could I not be?—but because I was so shaken by the discovery of my friend's dead body, somehow all my senses were not functioning normally."

"Lee walked up the few stairs."

Lee then looked at me and asked, "Gerald, are you all right, you look disturbed?" I nervously answered him, "You know Lee, I also had something strange happen to me." I began my story by reaching for one of my files, and asking him, "Did Lillian live at this address, and was her phone number such and such?" After describing her address, Lee gave me an odd look of amazement." Yes, yes, Gerald, that's Lillian. Did you also know her?"

I told Lee that I had called and spoken to Lillian on the phone the previous Monday. A month before she had asked me to design an inexpensive business card and letterhead logo for her. Because of personal issues, she had assured me she was in no rush, and had asked me to take all the time I needed. I had called her on that Monday at 3 p.m. to inform her that the work had been completed, and she needed to give a final approval on the job before it could be printed. Lillian had said, "I'll have to first take care of some 'loose ends.' I'll be by your office sometime before the week is up." If Lillian had died on the Friday morning, then I had definitely spoken to her three days after Lee had found her in her home dead!

Lee and I were speechless. At the time there was nothing either of us could say that would make sense, other than to acknowledge that Lillian's spirit was conducting business as usual, and was not ready to pass on to the "other side."

At the time of Lee's visit to my home, Lillian was scheduled to be buried in two days. I decided to attend the funeral with Lee.

After the funeral, when we arrived at my home, I told Lee that I was going to get rid of the work I had completed for

Lillian. I needed to clear my mind. I gathered all the paperwork, walked to the backyard, and put everything into the trash dumpster in the alley. I spoke softly, asking Lillian that I hoped she was satisfied with the logo I had designed for her, and that she did not need to pay me a "home visit" because as far as I was concerned, her account was paid in full!

Thankfully, I've not had any ghost activity at my house, or anything on a "spooky" level. But I have to admit that from time to time when my office phone rings, a little hesitation comes over me. Will a living person be at the other end, or a voice from beyond?

Chinese Camp

Years before the name Chinese Camp was established there was an earlier mining camp in the area, just one mile east, known as Camp Salvador. This camp was named after a group of Salvadorans who were both working the placers and prospecting for gold. Change came in the year 1849, when about 35 Cantonese miners arrived at Camp Salvador and also began prospecting. Chinese Camp became one of the many settlements to claim rich gold deposits.

Unknown to this day are the origins of these hardworking Asian fortune seekers. It has been speculated that upon arriving at San Francisco's port, a ship's Chinese captain brought his entire crew with him to the mines, abandoning his ship at port in search of greater wealth inland. There is another account that claims these landless laborers were hired by affluent English speculators to search for gold.

As news spread about the rich gold claims in the area, white miners soon arrived at Camp Salvador with a vigorous and aggressive determination to expel the Chinese. The American camp known locally as Camp Washington, or Washingtonville, was located opposite Camp Salvador, near Rocky

Hill. This small community, in an unusual move, received willingly the Chinese miners. Good fortune played its card and soon Camp Washington was a camp rich in gold ore.

Feeling relatively safe, more Chinese miners came and began to gravitate to, and eventually established, a large community of their own kin. And due to their patience and strong work ethic, the work claims that had been abandoned by the white miners as too difficult were used to build a successful Chinese community. During the mid-1850s, a population of around three to five thousand settled in the area. The placer mines produced more than $2. 5 million in gold.

As it grew, the camp became known by names such as Chinese Diggins', Chinee, and Chinese Camp. On April 18, 1854, a post office was established at the settlement and the name Chinese Camp was made official. Today, the one and only reminder of Chinese Camp's earlier history as Camp Washington lies in one of its roads' names—Washington Street. Today, a passing motorist barely glances at Chinese Camp. The community is humble, quiet, and small.

ROBERTA ANDERSON'S STORY

It's now been more than six years since my experience with a ghost took place. I was a recently divorced mother with a five-year-old daughter, Suzanne. One sunny day, Suzanne was playing by herself outside the house. Between our house and the neighbors was a small, shaded, concrete garden path where Suzanne enjoyed spending lots of time. This path, that connected my house with our neighbor's, was completely fenced. Even though I always kept a close watch on her. I never had any reason to fear that Suzanne would wander away, or leave the yard without my knowledge.

On both sides of the concrete path were beautiful five-feet-tall cana lilies. I watched as my daughter would spend hours playing among the base of these garden plants, using such sim-

cana lilies

ple things as tiny sticks to represent people, and small stones to represent houses. She gave the sticks names and actually preferred playing with these natural "toys" over her dolls, or other store-bought toys.

Suzanne was not an unhappy child. But I did begin to notice a subtle change taking place. A change that just did not sit well with me. A peculiar change that caused me to think that something was not right.

One morning, after breakfast, even though the weather was still much too cold for her to be outdoors, she asked me to let her go outside to play. She also stated that she did not want to watch her usual morning cartoons on television. I thought this request was very unusual for her, because she enjoyed her cartoons. Eventually, I did allow her to venture outside.

Throughout the morning I would glance out a window and check on her activities. I'd watch her lying on her stomach as she conversed with the rocks and sticks, laughing and giggling. What a sweet and trouble-free child, I thought to myself. Just a few ordinary rocks and sticks were all she needed to entertain herself.

When Suzanne came into the house, I noticed that she quietly went into the bathroom to wash her hands, then without turning on the television, she plopped herself on a chair in the living room. Sensing something was wrong, I walked over to her and asked, "Suzanne what are you thinking about?" She answered, "I can't play any more because the stinky man is mad at me." I said, "Suzanne what stinky man is mad at you?" She answered, "He told me he lives in the ground under the house."

Without immediately knowing why, a sense of uneasiness came over me. I asked, "Honey, what is this man's name and when have you seen him?" Suzanne answered, "I don't know his name, because he doesn't want to tell me his name, so I just call him the stinky man because he smells bad."

With a little fear in my voice, I sternly told Suzanne, "I don't want you playing outside anymore. I don't want you getting dirty, and talking to a stinky man anymore." Suzanne promised not to go outside again. I also noticed a hint of fear in her voice, which made me even more nervous. I sat next to her and gave her a hug. She said, "Mommie, do you think the stinky man will stay mad at me?" Her question caught me off guard. I said, "No, no baby, there's no man that's mad at you." Suzanne got quiet and then asked me if she could watch her cartoons.

About four days later, as I walked past the living room, I glanced at the open front door and caught sight of Suzanne sitting on the front porch speaking in a low whisper. I slowly approached her, and asked, "Baby, who are you talking to?" Suzanne looked up at me and said, "Mommie, what's a 'pitch'?" "A 'pitch'?" I answered. "I don't know honey, I don't know what a pitch is, why are you asking?" Suzanne answered, "The stinky man said that I'm a little pitch."

Startled by this I said, "Where did you hear that Suzanne, why did the stinky man call you a little pitch?" She answered, "He said that if I don't go outside to play with him, then I'm a little pitch." I never used profanity in front of my daughter, and my friends were not the type to use profanity in my presence, or in the presence of children. I was seriously concerned about finding out who this "stinky man" was.

I asked, "Suzanne, where is the stinky man now?" Pointing in the direction of the grapevine, Suzanne answered, "He's over there, looking at us. He's standing over there by the water hose." I looked and saw no one. I said, "Suzanne, I don't see a man." She answered, "He's standing there mommie, look. He's turning

"I saw the leaves on the vine move."

around now," she said. For the first time in my life, I got a cold chill that made me shiver to the bone.

I looked at the spot where Suzanne was pointing, about 20 feet away, and suddenly I saw the leaves on the vine move as if someone had brushed against them! There was absolutely no one in the area, and there was no wind. Suzanne quickly said, "Look mommie, he's leaving!" I had chills up and down my spine. I knew something was not right with this. I knew there had to be a reasonable explanation, but I could not think of one. I saw the leaves move, and could see that my daughter's reactions were genuine. But there was no visible person anywhere to be seen. Were we both imagining things? I don't think so. There was a ghost hanging around my daughter!

I took hold of my daughter's arm and bent down to look directly into her eyes, and asked, "Suzanne, how long have you been talking to the stinky man?" Before she could answer, a loud "thud" startled us. A small black bird had flown and hit the window we were standing near. It fell dead to the ground. I began to shake.

I know Suzanne sensed the fear in my voice because she told me she was scared. I asked her about the stinky man once again and she said, "He's still mad at me. I told him my Mommie said I couldn't go outside, and he said I was a little pitch." I said, "Suzanne, I want you to not ever speak to that man again, and I want you to tell me if you ever see him." She said, "Okay, I promise." I told Suzanne that I no longer wanted her to go outside the house unless I was with her. I told her that from now on, if she wanted to play, she would have to stay inside the house and watch cartoons.

I had mixed feelings about what she had told me about the man, the bad language he had spoken to her, and the movement of the vine's leaves. I felt both fear and anger at this ghost. I decided to talk to someone, so I gave my girlfriend a call at her office. Having described the details of the ghost to her, she told me, "Anne, you know how kids' imaginations can get the better of them. They talk to their dolls, and make up stories all the time. I don't see why you're believing in such nonsense. Maybe Suzanne is lonely for other playmates, or maybe she wants a sister or a brother. I don't see any harm in her making up imaginary friends."

When I reminded my friend about the moving leaves, the dead bird, and the words "little pitch," she said, "Well Anne, I don't know about that, but you know how kids pick up things from watching TV. But if there is a neighbor, a man that you are not aware of, talking to Suzanne, and using profanity, you need to find out who this guy is, and keep him far away from your daughter."

That night at around 8:30, I tucked Suzanne into bed, and then I went into the living room to watch some television. At about 10 p.m., I walked into the kitchen to make a snack. I decided to serve myself a slice of pie. I opened the refrigerator door and after reaching in for the pie, I placed the pie on the kitchen table, and turned around to get a knife. Suddenly, I caught the scent of something strange. Something that I can only describe as having a vinegar-like scent. Thinking there was something spoiled in the refrigerator, I opened the refrigerator door and took a sniff. Nothing. I closed the door, and as I turned around to face the table, my eyes caught the shadow of a person on the wall. This shadow was being cast by a person's body walking between the light from the television and the wall. I was scared.

I held my breath, and stared at the shadow for a few moments as it moved from one side of the room to the other. Instinctively, my fear turned to anger and I spoke out, "Damn you, calling my daughter a 'little bitch'. You leave her alone!" Without waiting for an answer, my instincts gave me the strength to rush to Suzanne's room. I opened her bedroom door, and as I entered, I could smell the same strange and unusually strong, foul scent I had smelled in the kitchen—it was now in Suzanne's room!

"He's right there, Mommie. Right there!"

As I entered the bedroom I saw Suzanne sitting upright in bed. I said, "Suzanne, are you all right, what are you doing up?" Suzanne answered, "The stinky man wants me to go outside and play with him. I told him I can't go outside when it's dark." My skin turned to ice. I turned the light on by her bedside table, and sat down next to her. "Suzanne," I said, "Where is this man now?" Suzanne pointed towards the direction of the room where I had hung a small basket of dried flowers. "He's right there, Mommie. Right there!"

Deep within my core, I felt the fear of coming face to face with this ghost. Even though I knew something paranormal was happening, I didn't want to scare my daughter anymore than she already was. I had never encountered anything close to this. I felt like running out the door, but my inner, motherly instinct took control. I turned to Suzanne and asked her in a controlled, calm voice, "What's he doing over there?" She answered, "He's not happy, Mommie. I told you, he wants me to go outside and play." Before I could ask Suzanne another question, the small basket on the wall with the flowers fell to the floor. I quickly stood up and took my daughter in my arms saying, "Come baby, you're not going to sleep in this room tonight." I shut the door to Suzanne's bedroom, and that night we both slept in the living room with the television and every one of the house lights turned on.

I awoke the next morning at about 7 a.m. Suzanne was still asleep at the foot of the couch, covered up to her chin with her favorite blanket. I walked to the kitchen and started the coffee maker. A few minutes later, I went into the bathroom and while in the bathroom, I heard my daughter's voice break the silence, "Mommie, the stinky man's here!" I flew out of the bathroom and found Suzanne sitting on the couch.

I asked Suzanne what had happened and where he was. She answered, "He was pulling my arm, Mommie. He wants me to go outside, he hurt my arm." I looked at Suzanne's left upper arm and saw the fresh red marks of three fingers. I had had enough of this ghost. Then and there I decided to get dressed and get out of the house.

As I walked quickly to my bedroom with Suzanne at my side, we walked past Suzanne's bedroom door, and noticed it was now wide open. I knew that I had made sure the night before to close it, and now it was open. I got dressed quickly, then dressed Suzanne, and we both got into the car. I drove the few miles to my father's house in nearby Jamestown. After describing my experience, and seeing the still-red finger marks on Suzanne's arm, my father demanded that we stay with him until everything could be sorted out.

The following day I left Suzanne with a friend as I gathered up cardboard boxes and returned to the house with my father and his next door neighbor, Chuck. I had made up my mind to move out of the house. The three of us entered, and completely cleaned out the house. Susan and I moved in with my father in Jamestown, where we have been living ever since.

There has been only one other strange thing that has

happened to us since our move. Two nights after we moved into my father's house, at about 9 p.m., an elderly neighbor named Arnold who lived across the street from us in Chinese Camp phoned to tell me that he had seen a strange man sitting on the stairs of my old house. Arnold knew absolutely nothing about our ghost experience. He described this man as having smooth, dark olive skin and thick, bushy eyebrows. The man wore a thin, dull-green colored shirt with matching trousers, and was somewhere in his late 40s. Arnold, cell phone in hand, walked over to the man. He asked the stranger what he was doing sitting on the stairs. The man responded, "I'm waiting for a little girl." Arnold, who's instincts gave him an uneasy feeling about this stranger had said, "Well, you better be on your way, or I'll call the sheriff." The stranger had stood up, and without saying anything more, walked away towards the highway. Arnold had noticed that the stranger smelled strongly of trampled, bitter weeds.

Arnold kept a close eye on this guy as he walked away, making sure he left the property. As soon as he reached the highway, Arnold, deciding not to take any chances, had phoned the sheriff. Arnold watched as the stranger stood next to the stop sign by the road. The man turned and faced Arnold. He just kept staring at Arnold. Soon, the lights of the sheriff's car came into view, completely passing the strange guy standing at the stop sign as the car drove up to Arnold's house. The sheriff asked Arnold where the stranger was. Arnold, who was puzzled, said, "What do you mean, you just drove past him over there by the road." The sheriff and Arnold then both walked toward the highway to the fence post. They found no evidence of the man. Arnold said he was amazed because he had been watching this guy all along. He never removed his eyes from the stranger. Now there was no sign of him. I described to Arnold the whole story of why my daughter and I had moved so abruptly two days before.

I never returned to the house. I even let my landlord keep my last month's rent deposit. No way was I going back into that house. I don't know the history of the house and I don't care to know. I have not brought up the subject to my daughter and thankfully, she has not had any after effects from the ghost incident. It's just as well.

Murphys

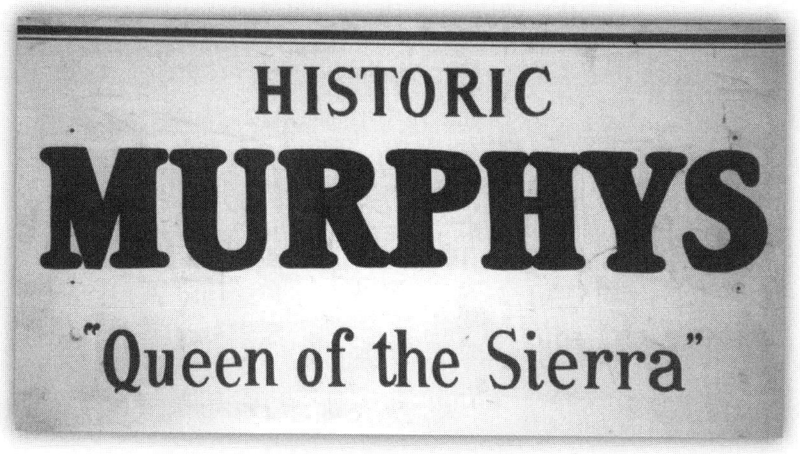

HISTORIC

MURPHYS

"Queen of the Sierra"

The year was 1848 when brothers Daniel and John Murphy, from whom the town got its name, came to the area. Rumor has it that the brothers were clever to a shrewd end, as they sold supplies and traded goods to the local miners at inflated prices. Their double-dealing trading practices did not end with their fellow miners, but instead increased in malice as they exploited local Native Americans as cheap labor. The brothers owned joint mining claims in the area, and in no time, became very wealthy as a result of the huge quantity of gold ore that was extracted from their mines.

Many notable names in history have visited Murphys, such as President Ulysses S. Grant, Horatio Alger, Charles Bolton (a. k. a Black Bart), and Mark Twain. Murphys is unusual in that it is celebrated for its climate that closely duplicates the wine-growing regions of France. As a result, there are several wineries located within a four-mile radius of Murphys' main street that have established themselves as superb and spectacular facilities.

Today, Murphys offers many natural attractions and antique stores. Art galleries and beautiful rolling hills are a visual feast for all. Events not to be overlooked are the annual Irish Days and Christmas Open House celebrations.

Arron Kregger's Story

I was born and raised in Chicago until the age of 24, then I moved to Decatur, Illinois, for three years. Deciding that I needed a major change, I moved to the country of Belize where I started a small juice bar business. This business lasted for five years, then I decided to move back to the United States, to Los Angeles, California, were I got a job working for the American Cancer Society. I remained employed at ACS for a little less than two years, when I got news of the death of my father.

My father had willed me $165,000. With this money, I decided to leave the big city of Los Angeles and settle in a much smaller community. I had visited the gold rush area of Northern California and was quite well acquainted with Murphys. I had always dreamed of living in this little town, so when the opportunity presented itself, I decided to buy a property in the area. Since then, I've lived in Murphys for close to 20 years.

As for my experience with a ghost, that happened to me while I was still living in Los Angeles. And, as you'll see, it eventually it followed me up here to Murphys.

The start of my experience took place within the same month I left Los Angeles. I remember the day being very sunny and hot. I was employed at the American Cancer Society and was on my lunch break. It was toward the end of my lunch hour that I looked at my watch and saw that I had about 10 minutes left. I decided to walk down Wilshire Boulevard, which is a major boulevard in Los Angeles. I walked for about a block, when I saw some commotion taking place up ahead of where I was going.

When I arrived at the scene, a small crowd had gathered at the intersection and I could hear a male voice yelling obscenities. I soon spotted the mentally deranged guy standing next to a mailbox, and he appeared to be out of control. He looked to be in his 40s, was unkempt, and gave the impression of being a homeless person. He kept yelling, "Hitlers, all of you are Hitlers, don't think I don't know what you want to do to me. I know, you want to kill me don't you? You want to kill me!"

Some of the onlookers were laughing and were amused at this guy's crazed behavior. In his arms he clutched a doll, and when I took a closer look, it was the "Snow White" Disney character doll. I felt sorry for this person. Obviously he was not mentally stable and needed to be looked at by a psychiatrist. Also, because of the recent news about my father's death, I guess I was feeling somewhat emotionally sensitive, so I decided to reach out to this guy. The crowd's reaction was so cruel. Since no one was making any attempt to help him, I decided to make a move, approach, and communicate with him. I didn't think much about what might happen. I wanted to sincerely reach out to a fellow human being. As I made a move toward him, his eyes immediately focused on me. I could see that he was not responding like I imagined he might, because he started yelling at me. I thought it was worth a try to keep approaching this guy, to bring him into reality by talking to him in a calm tone. No one else was attempting to help him, so I decided to keep trying. I took a few steps closer toward him, I extended one hand, and with the other made a waving motion for him to come on over to me. He turned to face me and started yelling, "Get away Hitler, get away Hitler!" I answered, "I'm trying to help you, I'm not Hitler. Do you need help? What's your name? How can I help you?" What happened next took place so quickly, to this day I can't remember the full details. It's all just a big blur to me. All I remember is that this guy turned away from me, then ran into the street, and a passing car hit him. As I said, I don't remember much after that. I just remember hearing screams, sirens, and people crying. I was totally confused, and everything since then has remained a blur. I do remember being interrogated by the police on the spot, while many witnesses gave their testimonies of what happened. The cop who wrote down my version informed me that I might be given a call to give further information. He presented me with his business card and told me to give him a call if I had any more information I could offer, but I never did. Since that day, I have never heard from the police again. As soon as the paramedics arrived on the scene, they began to work on the guy, and after a few minutes they placed a sheet over the body. As I said before, I was emotionally numb. It was a welcome relief to move out of Los Angeles when I did, given all the tragic events and memories of that terrible day. I've attended therapy sessions to help me cope with the guilt. The sessions have helped, but you never really get over something like that. I know I did the best I could, and shouldn't blame myself, but knowing is one thing, convincing myself has been quite another. My therapy sessions were basically all

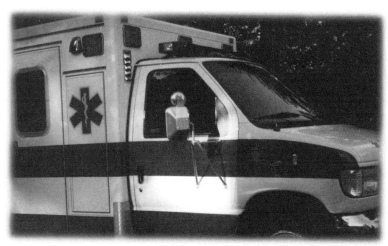

"The paramedics arrived on the scene."

about the guilt I needed to work through. I had some success, but I still carried the vision of that instant when the guy turned away from me and ran into the street.

After moving into my new house in Murphys, I began to have recurring nightmares about the accident. I would wake up at about 3 a.m. each morning and repeat the whole tragic scenario, over and over in my mind. Eventually I would get so tired and sleepy that I would fall back to sleep. I tried herbal remedies, over-the-counter medications, exercise, you name it. Nothing seemed to work for very long. Soon I sought out a psychologist, and was placed on antidepressants and prescribed sleep medication. They did help, but just when I thought I was going to get over this, things began to get worse. I began to notice strange noises during the night. At first I convinced myself that the noises were being made by the house settling. This is a very common occurrence; creaking noises are made when temperature changes take place, from daylight to night, and back again. This affects the wood framing of an older house, especially when the house is an older one, such as the one I had bought. But these sounds were different. The sounds I heard resembled the noise that is made when a piece of heavy furniture is dragged across a wooden floor. All the floors in the house were carpeted, so I was unsure if this was all in my imagination or not. The noises were coming from the living room, and once they began, they didn't last longer than about 30 seconds or so. I was concerned that it might be a loose water pipe, or some animal in the crawl space beneath the floor. Anything was possible. I never would have suspected in my wildest dreams that a ghost would be the cause of the noise. I was not too anxious to crawl under the house with a flashlight. The possibility of getting bit by a spider or a snake frightened me more than anything else I could imagine. Each night the same loud noise would begin, and after a few seconds, end. Somehow I got the idea that if I left a small lamp turned on in the living room, before going to bed, this might cause the noise to stop. Perhaps I was more concerned about just having the comfort of a light, a small excuse for not admitting to being a bit scared. At the time it made sense to me. That night, at the usual time, I was awakened by the noise. While lying in bed my eyes were wide open as I stared into the darkness. The dim light coming from the living room was reassuring as the noise got louder and louder. I must have been awake for about 10 minutes before something caught the corner of my eye. From the bottom of the door, from the narrow slit of space between the door and floor, I could see that something was moving about in the living room, because I was able to clearly see the shadow that is created when someone walks in front of a light. Someone was in my house, prowling about in my living room! As I got out of bed I tried to be as quiet as possible. I put my ear to the door and tried to hear something. I didn't hear a thing, so I grabbed the knob and quickly opened it. There in the room was the shadowy figure of a man seated on my sofa! I stood frozen in place, overcome with terror. Sweat was beginning to drip down my face and I was in shock. There was no doubt that this thing I was staring at was a ghost. The ghost's image was surrounded in a foggy, amber-color light, that

"The time was 4:10 a.m."

appeared to outline the ghostly man's image. Although I could not make out the details of his face, I did see that he was holding on to a doll. My stomach was in knots. I watched as the seated ghost slowly leaned toward me and clearly spoke the words, "Thank you." The last thing I remember is grabbing the side of the bedroom door with both hands, sliding to the floor, and fainting. Some minutes later, when I awoke, I remember crawling to the kitchen and pulling myself up to the sink. After I threw water on my face, I walked to the bathroom and looked at myself in the mirror. I was a mess. I looked at the small clock on the shelf; the time was 4:10 a.m. It wouldn't be long before the sunrise. I decided to get dressed, go outside, and take a walk. I knew I had been visited by the ghost of the guy who I had tried to help several months before, and I wanted to get out of the house quickly.

During my walk, I began to think over what I had experienced. Suddenly the words "Thank you"—the two words the ghost had spoken to me—hit me like a stone, and a feeling of joy and comfort filled me. I can't explain the total joy that came over me at that moment. I knew the guy who I had tried to help in Los Angeles, and who had been hit and killed by the car, had paid me a visit. More importantly, I knew that I was going to be okay. It all became clear to me. I knew that the ghost was not holding any grudges against me. My eyes began to fill with tears and I kept repeating out loud, "I'm so sorry, I'm so sorry." I knew I was going to be fine from now on. I made the decision to turn around and return home. I was not scared or hesitant in

any way. The sun was already up in the sky, and at that moment, the world was the most beautiful place to be. Since that day I've not had any further sleepless nights. Or any noises, or further visits from the ghost. He made his peace with me, and I made mine with him. I know that I'm a very lucky man. Well, that's my story.

THE HOUSE ON FRENCH GULCH ROAD (MEGAN WENTWORTH'S STORY)

I've lived in Murphy since the age of nine months, and I've heard that there are many homes and businesses that are haunted in the area. I was told that the Murphy Hotel has some ghostly activity that continues to this very day. This particular haunting is due to the murder of a man who was killed many years ago. Apparently his body is buried somewhere on the hotel grounds, but this is just one of the many stories I've heard growing up. One property that I know for a fact is haunted is my own home. The property on which our home is built is definitely, without a doubt, an activity center of ghostly occurrences. The name of the

"Mr. Stanton is buried somewhere in the old town cemetery."

original owner of our property was Oliver Stanton. Mr. Stanton was known locally by the strange name of "the Goat Man." My family was told that this nickname was given to him because of the hundreds of goats he owned, which he let run loose on the property. Strangely, when my family moved onto the property, there was an old goat still living on the property. It stayed on our property for about three years, until one day it just disappeared. People who knew the Goat Man have told us that he was a very private person who always kept to himself. Some have hinted to say he was also somewhat insane. Another rumor we've heard is that he also had a cache of gold buried on his property, in a location known only to him. I know that Mr. Stanton is buried somewhere in the old town cemetery. I myself have visited the cemetery attempting to locate his grave, but I've not been able to find it. My parents have asked some of the neighbors if they have a photo of Mr. Stanton, but no one has come forward with one.

After moving onto the property, we found numerous personal items that belonged to Mr. Stanton. An old barn was filled with antique farming tools, personal papers, etcetera. Prior to our purchase, the property had been abandoned for many years. People just stayed away from it, and I imagine this was due to the Goat Man's strange reputation.

Before our main house was built on the property, for several months my family lived in the original, smaller cabin fronting the road. During our stay at this cabin is where, as a child, I experienced my first en-

"This cabin is where I experienced my first encounter."

counter with a ghost. I remember one evening, as I entered the living room, I saw an old man sitting on our couch looking right at me. He was rather tall and lanky. His face had a very weathered look. He was wearing a long shirt, buttoned to the neck, and old jeans, and didn't speak a word to me. The very odd thing was the overwhelming scent of chicken soup that immediately filled the room. I've never understood why, but I could smell the strong scent of seasonings, or herbs. I know this sounds funny and strange. I've never thought of a reasonable explanation for why this stranger would be in the house. After staring at him for a short time, I turned around and walked away, not bothering to ask him who he was. Some time later I mentioned the man to my mother, who told me she was unaware of any visitor being in our house. She said that I should forget about the whole encounter, and so I never brought it up again.

As the months went by we eventually moved into the completed main house, up on the hill, where I experienced even more ghostly activity. One night, at about 11 p.m., my best friend Rachel and I got into our beds. Very soon after something caught our attention. I know this might sound crazy, but we both spotted a green, circular light, with a soft-yellow glow,

The main house

beginning to form on the floor of the room. We were amazed, scared, and speechless. The green light began to move up and around the wall, then it moved to the closet where it disappeared. That was the one and only time I experienced that green light. It never appeared to me or any of my family members again. Another time, my friend Rachel and I were sitting on the couch watching television when we experienced something else. The blinds on the windows in the room were pulled halfway down from the ceiling. There was no wind outside or air blowing from a ceiling fan. Suddenly, one of the blinds began to shake back and forth with enough force to hit hard against the window. All the windows in the room were securely closed and locked, so as I said before, there was no wind causing this activity. None of the other blinds were shaking, just this particular one directly in front of where we were seated. The blind continued its strange activity for about three minutes. My friend and I were totally fascinated. Once more, I mentioned what I had seen to my mother. This time she said that she could appreciate what I was experiencing, because she herself had experienced weird activity, and had even seen shadows of people moving about the house and walking up the stairs. Another time my boyfriend saw the shadow of a man walking outside the house. My boyfriend is 6'5", 250 lbs, and a mechanic by trade. He described a time while sitting at our kitchen table, when something caught his eye. He saw a dark figure slowly walk past the windows. He said the figure immediately gave him an ominous feeling. Since then, my boyfriend doesn't like being at the house by himself. He tells me the property gives him the creeps. Another evening two friends of mine, who had been staying at the property, were standing on the road, waiting for a car to pick them up and take them home. In the distance, they noticed the figure of a man walking up the road, toward the house. They kept their eyes fixed on this strange man as he slowly made his way toward them. When he got to within15 feet of them, he stopped, stood facing them, and then without saying a word simply disappeared! That's all, he just disappeared. Of course, they both ran back to the house and excitedly told me their story. I just got all freaked out. I knew they had just had an encounter with our ghost. Interestingly, whenever a ghost is seen on the property, it's always been in the shape of a man. Another example of the ghost inhabiting the house is its noisy footsteps. This, together with the strange door activity, is very common. We tend to hear footsteps, day or night, walking throughout the house. My father confessed that he used to hear the same footsteps in the cabin, before we moved, and now he also hears them in the new house. The doors in the house will make noises on their own, as if someone is grabbing hold of the knobs and giving them a good shake. We'll watch as a door will slowly begin to move, and then it shakes stronger and faster, until it rattles very loudly. It's as if someone is angry, or really wants to get our attention. Visitors to our house have reported hearing voices in the kitchen, when no one is around. One day my girlfriend was alone in the house, sitting in the living room. She suddenly began to hear someone's voice speaking out loud, and noisily moving things around, such as dishes and other items in the kitchen. Soon, she could hear the

sound of the refrigerator door being opened and closed. She decided to walk to the kitchen to investigate. Entering the kitchen she saw no one, but the strange thing was that the refrigerator door had been left wide open.

I own a pit bull who is a very mellow and sweet dog. She herself exhibits strange behavior toward the house. Many times something will grab her attention and she'll stare for hours at the stairs. This strange behavior really scares me. She'll just sit at the foot of the stairs, and focus for a long time at something invisible. I know that she sees the ghost of someone. I've heard that animals have the extra sense to see ghosts. Her behavior scares the "you know what" out of me! One time, I was seated on the living room couch, watching television. My dog was lying on my lap. When suddenly, she turned her head, and once again focused her eyes on the stairs. As I caressed her head, attempting to reassure her, I noticed that whatever she was looking at was agitating her to the point that she began to growl. Barking, she leaped off my lap, then ran to the stairs and growled at something that was invisible to me. Quickly, she ran up the stairs and barked some more, then she ran quickly downstairs and continued to bark at whatever remained at the top of the stairs. My dog's strange behavior is not something that only happens once in a while. This goes on all the time. There's something that likes to hang around those stairs that only she is able to see. It drives her crazy. These are the same stairs my mother mentioned to me where she has actually seen the ghost of a man walking up them. The footsteps are not only isolated to inside the house; we hear them following us around in our orchard. We hear the footsteps of someone stepping on the fallen leaves between the trees, and with each step we can hear them crunching on the gravel. The sounds are very obvious, and they are most often heard during daylight hours. The orchard is kept free of weeds, and the trees are regularly pruned, so it's easy to see between the rows. It has always given us a very weird feeling to hear these ghostly footsteps as they follow us through the orchard.

"We hear them following us around in our orchard."

For whatever reason, the ghost has chosen to linger on the property. I don't think he wants to hurt us. He likes hanging around our house—his old property. I know I've never done anything to cause the ghost of this man to come after me, but peculiar as it might sound, I'd like to actually see him. I think it might be interesting to know what he looks like and if he'd have anything to say. Aside from my own home, you also might be interested to know about the ghost that appeared at my place of work. I work at the Wild Rose and Mary, a flower and gift shop in town. It's also a hang out for the ghost of a man.

WILD ROSE AND MARY GIFT AND FLOWER BOUTIQUE

Historically, the small building used to be an actual working saloon. The present counter for the shop is the original saloon bar. Once we were told about a sad incident that took place in the store. A previous owner of the building visited the shop one day, and told us the story of the previous owners before him. Apparently, one of these owners had committed suicide using a gun, right next to where our present work table is situated. The visiting previous owner pointed out the bullet hole made in the wall, as it exited the man's body. He told us that for a time, the bullet hole was very visible. But because someone must have found the hole to be a gruesome reminder of the suicide, it had been covered with plaster and painted over. I used to be able to locate it easily on the wall, but now it's a bit more difficult.

One night, my boss Mary was at the shop, getting a floral work order for a wedding for the following morning. I was scheduled to come in that evening at 7:30 to help her with the order. When I walked through the door, I found her standing next to the flower work table with a strange look on her face. I asked her what was

"He was standing on the opposite side of the counter."

going on, and she explained that she had just experienced something very weird in the store. I asked Mary to explain and she said she had just seen a ghost. She said that while she was busy at the work table, the image of a man standing in the shop suddenly caught her eye. She turned to face the man at the opposite side of the counter, and noticed he was dressed in old-style clothes. He was holding a liquor shot glass, which he quickly raised to his lips, took a swallow, placed the glass on the counter, and then disappeared! Since experiencing the ghost, Mary has not seen any more ghosts, and doesn't seem to be bothered anymore by what she saw that morning. Just a part of living up here in a historical town, I guess.

MURPHY'S HOTEL AND LODGE

The Murphy's Hotel is a registered landmark and was originally owned by John Perry and James Sperry. These men opened the hotel in August of 1856 under the name Perry and Sperry Hotel.

Among the hotel's notable list of guests were Horatio Alger Jr., Mark Twain, Thomas J. Lipton, John Jacob Astor, J. P. Morgan, and former President Ulysses S. Grant. A great fire destroyed the town and hotel in 1859, but in March of 1860, the hotel was rebuilt and soon sold to Henry Atwood, who then sold it the following year to Harvey Blood, who sold it on to C. P. Mitchler, who renamed it the Mitchler Hotel. Mitchler died and the hotel was sold by his brother's widow to Mr. and Mrs. McKimens in 1945. They renamed it Murphy's Hotel. In 1963, the hotel was purchased by 35 investors who added the second story, as per the hotel's original design. Today, walking within this unique hotel is like taking a step back in time. The guest rooms are furnished with period antiques and have shared baths in keeping with the ambiance of 1856.

HEATHER BOWER'S' STORY

I began working at the hotel while attending high school. I started out as a bus girl in the dining room. Today I work the front desk. I'm very familiar with the hotel's stories associated with its ghosts and history. It's rumored that the second floor of the hotel is haunted by a male and female ghost. It's a wonderful place to work at, and the staff generally doesn't make it a point to mention our ghosts to new guests, especially when they are accompanied by small children. My first indication that there was a ghost haunting the hotel was when a hotel manager told me about the time she had been working the front desk and had been sitting right where I am now. Recalling her story still sends shivers up my spine. She told me that there had been nothing unusual about that particular evening. She had been on the phone taking a reservation when suddenly the antique chandelier directly above her had begun to sway in a slow, circular motion. In just a few seconds, it quickly and violently had moved with such force that it had broken free of the ceiling, electrical wires, and bolts! It had fallen down and crashed next to her, having missed her by just five inches!

Another employee, the hotel's banquet manager, also told me about the time she was in the banquet room, when a very weird thing had taken place. She described that as she had been finishing with, and straightening up, the room, she had pulled and closed all the heavy drapes covering the windows. Having done this, she had stepped out of the room for just a few min-

utes, but when she returned, she had
been shocked to find every one of
the drawn drapes torn from their
curtain rods and scattered about the
floor! She had been so scared by this
that she had refused to discuss the
event any further. She has since ex-
pressed to me that the experience
has made her uneasy, and to this
day, she doesn't feel very safe going
into that room alone. Just a couple
of weeks ago, the street directly in
front of the hotel was closed for re-
pairs. The hotel had very few guests
at the time. During one afternoon,
the housekeepers were all gathered
on the ground floor attending a
hotel meeting. I was seated behind
the desk. Not one person was on the
second floor. Well, as everyone was
gathered together, we soon began to
hear all these voices coming from

*"It began to sway in a
circular slow motion."*

the empty second floor. The voices were very loud and obvious,
and I had no trouble recognizing them as being the sound of a
man and woman engaged in loud conversation. It sounded as if
they were just at the top of the stairs. Keep in mind that the dining room is also on the second floor. The same dining room
where the drapery had been torn from the rods. No one was on
the second floor at the time. We all kept quiet, nervously listen-
ing to the voices. Soon they slowly faded away and we were all
left staring at each other in disbelief. Other common sounds
that employees continue to hear are the ghostly footsteps that
walk about the second floor. As I said, this is a common experience that never seems to go away. I've noticed that the footsteps

can be more commonly heard in the early morning hours. I begin work at the hotel at 6 a.m., and I've noticed that the ghosts start walking around at about the same time.

One historical incident that is well documented, and actually took place at the property, is the time a man was shot directly outside the main hotel entrance. His name was William Holt. Historically, Mr. Holt was one member of an old- time gang of bandits in the Murphy area. He was fatally killed as he was entering through the hotel's main entrance. His signature, written in his own hand, can be viewed in the hotel's registry. I don't have any way to prove if his ghost is the one that inhabits the hotel, but it makes sense to me. A friend of mine named Angela, who used to work at the hotel's front desk, spoke to me about a few incidents she had experienced at the hotel. Several times, while alone, and standing in the lobby, she had sensed the invisible presence of someone with her. She told me that this was the presence of a man. She could easily see by turning to look around the lobby that no one was in the room. But very soon after she could smell the scent of burning tobacco smoke. After a few minutes, this scent would leave, and a new scent of Lilac perfume would take over. She had had no explanation for this, but she had always felt that the hotel was, without question, haunted. One day, a maid approached Angela, asking if she would accompany her to room number 9 on the second floor. The maid was nervous and apprehensive about entering a guest's empty, unlocked room by herself. The door was apparently left open by the guest, and because of strict security issues, she wanted another staff member to serve as a witness, and accompany her when she entered the unlocked room. Both Angela and the maid walked upstairs and knocked on the door loudly announcing, "Housekeeping, anyone in the room?" When there came no answer, they walked inside. Looking around the room, and not seeing anyone, they decided to leave. When Angela grasped the knob, attempting to close the door, someone within the obviously empty room began to pull on the door! Apparently the ghost wanted it to stay open. A tug of war ensued, and after a few seconds, Angela, using a lot of force, shut the door and locked it.

The second floor of the hotel, to this day, still gives me a creepy feeling that is difficult to shake. I know that the ghosts of the hotel have never hurt anyone, but it's not easy for my mind to make that connection. Don't get me wrong, I do tend to enjoy "ghostly" things, reading books, and talking to people about the paranormal, so why would I fear actually seeing one of the

"The maid was nervous and unsure if she should enter the room."

ghosts? I guess it would freak me out at first, but crazy as it now might sound, I would indeed welcome such a visit.

OROVILLE

Oroville's non-Native American history begins with Gabriel Moraga, who had visited the area in 1808. Gabriel Moraga was followed by Spanish explorer, Captain Luis Arguello, who in 1820, noticing the many wild pigeon feathers floating on the river, named the river "Rio de las Plumas" or the River of Feathers. Ultimately, the river was renamed The Feather River. In 1848, anglo settler John Bidwell discovered gold along the river bank, thus starting a massive gold rush of fortune seekers. The birth of "Ophir City," a tent town, later became Oroville in 1856, which is Spanish for "City of Gold," and remains today the city's official name.

Oroville is filled with many historical sites and landmarks. Of particular note is the Ishi Monument dedicated to the memory of Ishi, the last known member of the Yahi Native American nation. The monument reads: "The Last Yahi Indian. For thousands of years the Yahi Indians roamed the foothills between Mt. Lassen and the Sacramento Valley. Settlement of this region by the white man brought death to the Yahi by gun,

This basket woven by Selena LaMarr in 1899 once belonged to Shavehead, Chief of the Hat Creek Atsugewi. Inspired by nature, this design represents "mok-co-wek-kee," or deer droppings.

by disease, and by hunger. By the turn of the century only a few remained. Ishi, the last known survivor of these people, was discovered at this site in 1911. His death in 1916 brought an end to Stone Age California."

IRENE LOBAIN'S STORY
Peter and I have lived in Oroville for 28 years. Our ghost experiences began a few weeks after my husband mother's death 15 years ago. Peter's mother, Mary, came to live with us in June of 1986 and died in September of that same year. Mary was diagnosed with cancer of the sinuses, which soon developed into a very invasive cancer. It was not long before the doctors had changed her prognosis to terminal.

Mary Lobain

Peter and I were both devastated by the news. However, Mary's overall attitude was surprisingly realistic and tranquil. Mary, the daughter of a Methodist minister, was born in Jamaica, and raised in West Virginia where she lived most her life. When she was diagnosed with cancer, most of her family and friends had preceded her in death. She had no family to care for her in West Virginia, so we decided to move her to Oroville. Not long after Mary's death and burial, Peter began to experience strange things in our home. Unusual shadows, voices, and unexplained images in mirrors. On one occasion, I also got to witness a ghost experience, which left me speechless. About two weeks after Mary's funeral, Peter was on the phone speaking to our banker one early afternoon, when he happened to glance out of the dining room picture window and catch the image of his mother standing next to our car. Peter explained that his mother's ghost was dressed in her favorite green dress, holding her white purse. Peter's impression of the visitation was that his mother's spirit was waiting to be driven into the town of Chico to do her shopping. Mary always enjoyed, and looked forward to, her Friday shopping trip with her son.

Peter told me he was left speechless by the image. Our banker sensed that something was not right because he asked Peter, "Are you all right, is every thing okay?" Eventually, Peter ended his phone call with the banker saying, "I need to take care of something, I'll call you later." Peter then turned around

"The ghost was holding her white purse."

and nervously described to me what he had just seen standing in the driveway. I was not convinced, and told him that his imagination was working overtime. He insisted that he had seen his mother standing by the car, but eventually he convinced himself that it must have been his imagination. We talked about the incident later that night before going to bed. I was concerned about his mental state, that he was feeling stressed or depressed. I said he needed to call our doctor to share what he had seen with him. Peter assured me he would do that the following week. Later that night, at about 4 a.m., I was awakened by the pressure of a hand on my forehead. I opened my eyes and in a few seconds I could smell my mother-in-law's familiar perfume. I froze! I knew there was something strange going on. I looked over at Peter, who was sound asleep. As I leaned back on my pillow, I could not let go of Mary's strong presence in the bedroom. I knew she was there in the room with us, I could just feel her. I kept my eyes opened and slowly scanned the dark bedroom. Sure enough, standing in front of the closet door appeared an elongated white light, the height of the door. The light hovered about three feet off the floor and did not move. It was a dim light that glowed bright, then dimmed, glowed bright again then dimmed. It gave me the impression of a silent heart beating very slowly, but without making any sound. With my eyes fixed on the light, I got the courage to speak in a soft voice, "Mary, it's time for you to leave us. It's time for you go on to heaven." The light kept glowing and the scent of perfume grew stronger. Peter suddenly awoke and asked me what was going on. I told him to look over toward the closet. "See that light over there?" I said. Peter's fumbling hand reached over to the night stand, searching for his glasses. By the time Peter had placed the glasses on his head, the light had disappeared.

Although the light had disappeared, I remained convinced that Mary was still in the house. For the remainder of that night, I was unable to fall back to sleep. Peter kept insisting that I repeat word for word what I had seen to him. I knew he was trying to make sense of what had appeared to me, but his nervous questioning was making me an emotional wreck. I told him that I needed to go to the kitchen and think about things. In a few hours the sun would be up, so I explained to Peter that I would have a much clearer mind to discuss everything I had seen over breakfast. Peter remained in bed until 8 a.m. That morning we both discussed what I had seen and what it all might mean. Could the glowing light that I had seen actually be Mary's ghost? Could there possibly be another explanation for the lights, perhaps the headlights from a passing car? Or, do I have an overactive imagination? So many possibilities crossed my mind, but in my heart I knew that what I had seen was not something that could be explained in normal terms. And what about the scent of Mary's perfume? I still could not think of a 100 percent explanation that satisfied me. I remained convinced

"We both stood, our eyes fixed on the cup and spoon."

that it was actually Mary's spirit who had visited my husband and me. For the remainder of the day, Peter and I went about our normal daily routine. But try as I might, Mary's visit the night before was very difficult to erase from my mind. I decided to take a drive into town and do a bit of shopping. When I returned to the house, I walked directly into the kitchen and placed my bags on the table. I turned to open the the door to the pantry when I noticed something on the sink counter. It was Mary's favorite coffee cup, and lying next to it was a small teaspoon. I called to Peter who was in the living room watching television, "Peter, were you going to use your mother's coffee cup for something?" He said, "No, why?" I told him to come to the kitchen immediately. We both stood, our eyes fixed on the cup and spoon. He swore he hadn't taken it out of the cupboard, and I know I hadn't. The hair on the back of my neck began to stand on end. I knew that Peter would not have any reason to make up such a thing for the purpose of scaring me.

Without any further thought I said, "Peter, because of everything you and I have been experiencing, I think your mother wants to tell us something. I think she wants us to wish her a good journey. I think you should communicate, tell her out loud that it's okay to leave the house, that you'll be fine." Peter gave me a strange look, but realizing I might be making sense, he reached out to grasp my hand and said, "Mother, go on to heaven. Everything will be okay with Irene and me." The next thing that happened might sound crazy, but it did happen, I swear it did! Right after my husband uttered those words we heard Mary's soft voice respond out of thin air, "Love you." I nervously let go of Peter's hand and embraced him. He began to cry and I felt happy knowing everything would be fine from that day on. I just knew Mary would be happy now. Nothing more has taken place to indicate Mary is still in the house. The experience gave me a certain courage and a new belief about the existence of spirits. I was a non-believer, but no longer. Four years ago on April 12, 1997, my husband left me. He died suddenly from a heart attack. Sure I miss him very much, but because of the experience with Mary's spirit, I know that Peter's spirit is now with his mother, and that they are both doing well. This gives me comfort during those times when I miss him so much. I really do believe this. I haven't had any visits from Peter, or his Mother. I know we go on to a better place when we die, but only if we do the right things on Earth. Thank you for allowing me to tell you about what I experienced. I hope my story will bring peace to someone.

OROVILLE CHINESE TEMPLE AND GARDEN

Listed in the National Register of Historic Places and as a California Landmark, the Oroville Chinese Temple once served a community of 10,000 Chinese. In 1949, during California's Centennial, it officially opened its doors to visitors.

CISSY SANT'S STORY

As of today I've worked at the temple for over six years, as its caretaker and tour guide. Prior to my employment at the temple, I was unaware of any ghost-like activity on the property. No one ever came to me with any information about it being haunted. But all that slowly began to change. Before I tell you about my personal experiences with the spirits at this site, I'd like to begin with a short history of this unique and historic temple. The first temple was built in 1863, and served the spiritual needs of the 10,000 Buddhist, Taoist, and Confucian Chinese population of the area. The English translation of the name of the temple is "Temple of Many Gods." Notably, it is quite unusual to find three distinct religions being practiced together in the same complex. As such, it remains the West's largest, authentically furnished Chinese temple and the largest of its kind and of its era.

In 1868 a two-story building was built directly behind this first temple. The Buddhists used the large, second-floor room, with its large circular doorway, as a prayer room. They named

this prayer room "The Moon Temple." The Buddhists believe this circular doorway symbolizes the circle of life, eternity, and reincarnation. Beneath the Moon Temple, on the first floor, is the Counsel Chambers. This room was used by the Chinese as a type of "city hall." Decisions affecting their community, and other important issues, were regularly discussed here. Another interesting function of the room was that it also served as a funerary preparation room for the Chinese community. Located about two miles from the temple, on the southwest side of Oroville, is the original Chinese cemetery. It's located on Feather River Boulevard, just past the WalMart. It's easy to drive past this important and historic part of California's past. Its present, unassuming condition definitely belies its historical significance. After a body had been buried in this cemetery, it was left in the ground for about −10 years. Following this time, a chosen person from the Chinese community would disinter the body, clean the bones, and then bring them into the temple's Counsel Chambers where they would be religiously prepared for their return to China. The Chinese community in Oroville believed that if a member of their race died in a foreign country, on foreign soil, that person would not go to Heaven. Also, because of their traditional strong family bonds, family members back in China were morally responsible for the care, and for respectfully overseeing that the body and bones of the deceased were returned to his or her homeland.

In 1874 an adjoining room named "The Chan Room" was added to the temple. Initially, the room was built for the sole use of the Chan family for their private worship and ancestor prayer, but it also served as a community temple of Confucian teachings. The Chan family, aside from being Chinese, was one of the very few wealthy families in the area. The Chan's wealth was based on mercantilism. Initially, Mr. Chan arrived in the area to mine for gold, but he soon discovered that he could make more money, with less effort, by supplying the miners with retail goods.

Eventually, due primarily to the construction of the two newer temples, the original first temple became known as the Daoist Temple. Presently, within the original temple, are three wooden statues of Chinese Gods: Mulan (Woman Warrior), Huat'o (Doctor of Medicine—renowned as the first person to do surgery and who defined acupuncture, pulse points, and meridians), and Tien Hau (Goddess of the Sea, Queen of Heaven—protectress of sailors, prostitutes, and travelers in foreign lands).

An interesting point to note about Oroville's history are the many tunnels underneath the older part of town. Supposedly, the Chinese dug interconnecting tunnels underneath the town, and as recently as a few years ago, the supporting pillar of a private residence began sinking into the ground. I was told that

Cemetery grave markers

"A coldness would start to envelop me."

there was a large pit, 40-feet deep, under this house, with several side tunnels leading off, which joined others. I've also read stories of sections of Montgomery street collapsing under the weight of trucks, due to these tunnels. Now that you have a general idea of the temple's history, I'll begin with my own encounters with what I believe were spirits that made themselves known to me on the property. I recall one of the first experiences I had that caused me to think things were not "right." It was over a period of days when I would walk into the main temple and unusually cold chills would take over me. These chills were unusual because the days were warm, and I was not thinking of spirits or anything close to ghosts. Every time I would enter the temple a coldness would envelop me. This continued for quite a number of days. Eventually I believe the spirits got used to having me around, or I got used to them, because the chills stopped and I've not felt any since. On the other hand, I've had some visitors on my tour tell me that they have experienced these same chills.

Each week I conduct several tours throughout the day, and there are instances when some of the participants will exhibit unusual behavior. I'll spot someone visibly shake and shudder, and I'll ask them if they're okay. The response I'll get is that a cold breeze has just swept over them. I do believe that some people are more sensitive to unseen things than others. My response is to just shrug my shoulders and continue on with the tour. Admittedly, the temple can be a scary place for some, but I don't find it at all scary. Its definitely an unusual structure, given its old and exposed brick walls, and its altar as its focus. The exotically carved Chinese god figures might also add to the strangeness of the overall atmosphere. But I don't find anything in the temple to be uniquely scary in nature. Some months ago, I was visited by two ex-caretakers who asked me a weird question. I was asked if the spirits had begun playing with me. I was caught off guard by these questions, so I asked for a further explanation. I was told that when they had been alone in the temple's office they had sometimes felt the sensation of small, invisible fingers tickling and playing with their hair. The feeling of invisible fingers stroking the middle of their necks would continue at different times of the day. Feeling surprised, I answered that I had indeed had those same experiences, but I had chosen not to dwell on them.

I recall, very soon after I began working alone at the temple, that I had started to feel the sensations of being touched at the base of my neck. I rationalized that these tickling sensations were previously unnoticed spiderwebs and I had unknowingly walked through them. But there were instances when I would be alone, sitting down reading a book, when suddenly the tickling sensations would begin. I would start waving and batting my arms all around my head, attempting to remove what ever it was that was bothering me. I knew that I was experiencing something strange, but I just did not want to admit it. However, one particular day, I remember being in an unusually bad mood. Again, I was sitting in the office area when the tickling started. Being in a

"I'll turn and see shadows of people moving."

bad mood, I was in no mood for play, so I spoke to the spirit in a very stern voice, "Go away, leave me alone!" The tickling immediately left me, and ever since that time, I've never had another tickling experience at the temple. I've experienced other unusual little things in the temple, such as when our Open and Closed sign has turned on its own. I know that a spirit is playing with me, because at the end of the day, as I routinely lock up the temple, I've noticed on several occasions when I have turned the sign to its close position it will have been turned back to its previous position. I've never actually seen it physically turn, but the sign has always been turned when I am facing away. I'm a very fastidious and detailed person, so for this to happen over and over again bothers me. I've also seen people's shadows darting around the property. No matter where I'll be in the temple complex, some movement will catch my eye. I'll turn, and see the shadows of people, or just dark images, darting quickly about the area. These shadows most often appear in the courtyard area, just outside the Counsel Chambers.

Another fairly common experience for me has been the "voices" that I can hear coming from the temple. I'll be alone, sitting in the office which shares a common brick wall with the temple, and I'll hear low, whispering voices. I can't make out the words, or if they are speaking English or Chinese, but I know I am hearing the voices of two people in conversation.

My belief is that I'm open to ghostly experiences. I'm not afraid. I don't discount anything that I can't see as being unreal. I think that there are spirits here who are protecting their temple, who are making sure that each visitor is respectful. As the temple's caretaker, I'm required to live on the grounds, and I do feel protected by these spirits. Because I do see shadows, and hear the voices of spirits regularly, I've gotten to the point where I don't pay much attention to them any longer. This is their temple, and that's that. But, I've got to admit, that sometimes the voices do cause me to pause and think. It's interesting that most of my ghost experiences have taken place, or have been more prevalent, in the winter. Would I welcome an actual visit

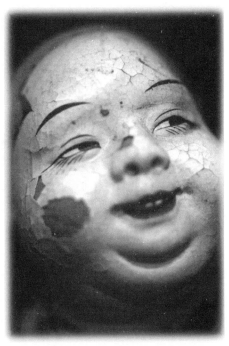

"I'll begin to hear low, whispering voices."

from one of the spirits? I guess I'd like to see what one of these guys looks like face to face. I know I'd be a bit startled at first, but other than that, maybe I'd enjoy the encounter.

GRASS VALLEY

Between 1848 and 1849 prospectors from Oregon in search of gold, along with emigrants from the East Coast in search of fertile land, settled in Grass Valley. To this day, many believe that millions of dollars of unmined gold ore lies undiscovered in and around the pleasant town of Grass Valley. Because of its abundance, gold played a key role in the area's population explosion. A well-told story tells of a miner who was one day searching the area for his lost cow. As he walked about the fields, he stubbed his toe upon a rock, dislodging it. As he picked up the rock, he noticed the unique and unmistakable sparkle of gold that had capped itself to the rock. This accidental stroke of fortune soon led to another fortuitous encounter for a man who was searching for stones to fashion a chimney for his new home. Among the stones in his collection were several covered in gold. Soon a staggeringly rich vein of gold ore was discovered, causing even more of a frenzy. In 1855 a devastating fire swept through the town and destroyed the 300-plus structures of Grass Valley. The town's people rallied together and rebuilt the town. By the 1860s more than $150 million in gold had been extracted from the two major mines—North Star and Empire. In 1956, both mines were closed, and today on their proper sites, the current City of Grass Valley has constructed both a public park and a museum.

Grass Valley today is renowned for its living museum, filled with early gold-rush period architecture, and thrives as a modern business center.

LEO OTT'S STORY

I was born and raised in Fresno, California. During my childhood, my parents enjoyed taking the family on visits throughout the Gold Rush Country. As I got older, and was able to drive a car, I found myself taking frequent trips on my own into this historic area of Northern California. I enjoyed the history and architecture of the area, and knew that when the opportunity

presented itself, I would one day make it my home. Nine years ago, after a major turn of events in my personal life, I decided to make the move from Fresno and settled in this area. At the time of my move I had a wonderful relationship with a man who unfortunately died in a motorcycle accident. I was devastated by the loss, and was going through a bout of depression. I needed to find a focus in my life. John and I were together for only two years, but I've never really gotten over the pain of losing him. I don't know if I'll ever fully recover from this loss. I imagine I sound as if I want pity, or for people to feel sorry for me, but on the contrary, I just want to let you know what I was going through at the time. Surprisingly for me, I've grown to enjoy the privacy and ease of doing things on my own. Before moving out of Fresno, I had studied yoga for five years and had become interested in following a healthy lifestyle, eating only vegetarian-based foods and eliminating milk and egg products from my diet. This change also prompted me to look at the direction in which my life was headed. I decided to make the move out of a large city, and when the time came to begin my search for a property, my focus was to locate a house, and land, that would give me the peace and quiet I needed. I searched around the area for weeks, looking to purchase a home and small acreage to start a business growing organic vegetables and flowers. In Fresno one morning, I was having coffee at a local bakery. As I read through a listing of available properties in a local paper, a description of a house in the gold-rush town of Grass Valley caught my attention. Grass Valley was not my first choice, but after reading the property's description, I knew I had to take a look. After driving the long highway and arriving at the property, I was not disappointed. The house was just what I was looking for, and the sloping four acres of land was perfect for growing plants. I moved in two months later and soon felt very comfortable in my new home. Living alone was at first difficult for me, but I soon got into the routine of doing the daily chores and such.

"My ghost experiences began during my first winter at the house."

As for my ghost experiences, they began during my first winter in the house. At first I rationalized it all as just my imagination, but it didn't take long for me to realize that there was something more complex going on. I recall the first time I noticed something strange taking place was in the bedroom. It was in November, and I was typing an email to a friend on the computer one afternoon, when I heard the sound of footsteps in the hallway. I had no doubt that there was someone in the house with me, because the footsteps were loud, and distinctly footsteps. I was startled, got out of my chair, and took a few cautious steps as I made my way to the bedroom door. I wanted to call out and ask who was there, but I thought it would be best to surprise whoever it was that had entered the house. Perhaps it was a visiting friend, or the real estate agent who had sold me the house. I searched the whole house and didn't discover anyone, or any evidence of anyone having entered the house. The front and rear screen doors were still latched from the inside. At that moment, something in me, an inner voice, said that things were not going to remain the

"I'm not ashamed to admit that I was terrified!"

same for me. I knew, and was convinced, that what I had heard was not my imagination. As the rest of the day progressed, I kept an ear open for sounds of any further "visits." Then a few hours later, the footsteps returned! This time I sat firmly in my chair. My hands were frozen in position over the computer keyboard as I held my breath. With each step, the footsteps made the old wooden plank floor creak. Slowly, the steps made their way to the room where I was seated. I heard them stop at my door. I turned apprehensively to face whoever, or whatever, would be standing at the door. I saw the smoky figure of a person. It was not a white form, as most people might imagine a ghost to be. Rather, this ghost was hazy and gray in color. I quickly stood up and I remember saying out loud, "Oh, God!"

I'm not ashamed to admit that I was terrified! I took a few steps back and let out a scream! The impression I had was that the ghost was neither friendly nor familiar. It was dark and ominous. Without thinking, I yelled, "Get out, get out of my house!" Immediately the ghost began to shrink into itself until it became a little sliver of black. It became a long strip of darkness that hung in the air for about 30 seconds, until it simply ceased to be visible. It had faded into nothingness! I stood there in shock. Slowly I got the courage to walk toward the door and into the hallway. I searched every area and room of my house.

Nothing was out of place. I looked at my wall clock—the time was 4 p.m. The day was sunny. I do not drink or do drugs. The only medication I use is for seasonal allergies, and that's it. I swear, I saw this thing come into my house and appear to me in broad daylight. The next incident took place just a couple of days after this one. I was outside hammering a garden-hose holder to the side of the house. I was coiling the hose around the holder, when I noticed movement in the yard. I glanced over at the porch and saw a man sitting on my porch chair! I was only about 20 feet away, and there was a leafless rose vine covering most of the porch, but I could see this man in his mid 40s, sitting on the porch staring straight ahead. I dropped the hose I was holding, and with command in my voice, spoke in his direction, "Can I help you?"

He turned his head toward me then disappeared. This all happened within the span of about five seconds. I had had enough. I was convinced that my house was haunted. There were ghosts not only in the house, but also existing on the property! I didn't know what to do about this. What was I supposed to do? I walked back into the house, grabbed a few clothes, my car keys, and drove to Fresno for the night. No way was I going to stay alone in the house. Arriving in Fresno, I spent the night at my cousin Duke's apartment. The next day I asked Duke, who was unemployed at the time, to come spend a week or a few days with me. Duke was intrigued with my ghost story, and he accepted my offer. His curiosity was definitely aroused and he excitedly said, "I'd enjoy having an encounter with a real ghost. After all, how many times does such an opportunity come up to spend a night at a haunted house." I spent one more day in Fresno, then the next morning Duke and I drove back to Grass Valley. Everything seemed normal and ordinary when we reached the house. No evidence of any ghostly activity as far as I could see. The front door to the house was locked, as I had left it. I started up the furnace and we both soon found comfortable positions in front of the

television. I thought to myself, no more ghosts. Please, no more ghosts.

We were watching the evening news when suddenly from the kitchen we heard the sound of a dish fall into the porcelain sink. The sound startled me so much, I jumped straight out of my chair! We stood, looking at each other, waiting for something further to happen. But nothing did. I cautiously walked to the kitchen and saw that a small serving dish was lying in the sink. I picked it up and returned it to the dish rack. Nothing unusual had happened that couldn't be explained, I thought. Just a dish that had slipped off the dish rack. That's all. I turned to walk back into the living room, saying to Duke, "No ghost, just a dish." Not more than a few seconds later, having sat back down in my chair, I heard once again the sound of a dish being moved, breaking the silence. I knew this was not normal. You had to be there in the room with us to see the frightened look that came over both our faces. Duke said, "Let me go take a look." As he walked to the sink, he reached inside and pulled out the same dish I had just placed on the rack. "That's impossible," I said. "You know I placed it on the rack. That dish could not have jumped back in the sink again like that on its own." Attempting to make light of the situation, Duke said, "We got a little 'poltergeist' thing going on here." He picked up the dish, gave it a quick look over, then placed it back in the sink saying, "Well Mr. Ghost, if you want to play house, go ahead, and enjoy yourself." Duke came back into the living room and we continued to watch the television. I remained nervous, but Duke did not seem to be bothered at all by the kitchen incident. His lack of concern must have transferred over to me, because soon I began to feel more at ease. I became sleepy and said, "Duke, I'm going to call it a night. You know where the blankets are, see you in the morning." That night I slept very lightly. Twice I heard Duke walk down the hall and make his way to the bathroom. I thought it was odd that he didn't flush the toilet, but then thought he hadn't wanted to wake me by making noise. Nothing I could call strange, or paranormal, took place during the night. However, the next morning I would change my mind. I was the first to wake up, and leaving my bedroom I walked into the bathroom. I could see that Duke had not used the toilet. When I went into the living room, I found him asleep on the couch. The television was turned on with the volume off, and he had also turned on the light on the desk by the front door. I spoke, "Duke, wake up. What are you doing asleep here in the living room?" He explained that not long after I had gone to bed, he had turned all the lights off except for the television. At about 11:30 p.m., he had heard a noise in the kitchen. He had turned to look, and had seen a guy leaning against the sink. He could tell it was a ghost because of the transparency of the figure. Speaking in a shaky voice, Duke had said, "What do you want. Don't hurt me." Duke said the ghost then had smiled at him and had disappeared! Duke had been shaken by the apparition, but had not wanted to wake me. Instead, Duke had decided to turn on the lights and had slept with the television on the rest of the night. I asked Duke why hadn't he just come over to my bedroom and waken me. He could have told me about the ghost that appeared to him when he got up twice to use the bathroom during the night. Duke looked at me and said, "What do you mean? I didn't use the bathroom at all last night. To get to the bathroom, I would have had to walk through the kitchen. I wasn't going to get up and take a chance of meeting up with that ghost again! Your house is haunted, Leo. I believe you. This house is definitely haunted!"

We both considered what to do next. Duke described the ghost in detail, but neither he nor I could identify who it might be. Finally, I made the decision to remain strong, and I told Duke that I was not going to leave and give up my house to a ghost. I was planning on staying for good. I made sure I spoke loudly, directing my words to the ghost. "One of us is going to have to leave the house, and it's not going to be me. So whoever you are, you better leave now!" Duke spent another night with me, and neither of us experienced another disturbance. Although we were both a little unnerved, things seemed to be going all right. I drove Duke back to his home in Fresno. All the while I was apprehensive about returning to my home. But I drew strength from my conviction that it was my home. After all, I did not want to let the ghost get the better of me. I had been through too much in my life to give up everything to some wayward ghost. Returning home, I walked into the dark living room, turned on the light, and said, "Look, I want to be at peace in my house. I hope you can understand this. I don't want to have to be on the lookout for you. I don't know what you want, but please, leave me alone to live my life. You've already lived yours, so you should go on and live your own life doing whatever you need to do. But do it somewhere else and leave me alone." I must have said something that the ghost understood, because as soon as I had finished saying the last word, I heard a loud "crack" sound. It was the sound that a breaking board would make. It was sudden and loud. It startled the heck out of me, but I knew this must be the answer to my firm declaration. The ghost heard me and respected my stand. Immediately, I felt the heavy atmosphere in the room change. Difficult as it is to try to explain, I felt that the ghost had left my house. I know I took a chance of angering the ghost, but it was after all my house. I couldn't keep spending nights in other people's homes. It was my house, and I was willing to fight to keep it!

It's now been a few years since all those occurrences took place, and nothing ghostly has since appeared to me in the house. I don't hear noises at night, or see shadows or dishes flying in the air. I am finally living a normal life, the life I have always wanted. One re-occurring question people have asked me when I tell them my story is, "Do you think the spirit you saw was your partner who died, and wanted to make contact with you?" My answer is that this ghost was definitely not related in any shape or form to John. I don't believe that loved ones want to come back and scare us. The ghost I experienced was a dark and mischievous one. As I said before, I was frightened and could feel the negative presence of this ghost. Love has a very different presence, a very different one from the one this ghost was presenting to me. I haven't had any more incidences and I don't want anymore. So far the ghost has stayed away.

MARIPOSA

In 1850, Mariposa occupied more then one fifth of the state of California, thus earning the name "Mother of Counties." It grew rapidly with the discovery of gold, and today the county covers 1,455 square miles. The town's name, Mariposa, is Spanish for butterfly. It was named by Gabriel Moraga. Butterflies would gather in clouds along the town's creek and, no doubt, provided Señor Moraga with the idea for the delightful name. John C. Fremont founded the town with a land grant, and in 1854 donated a portion of this land upon which today sits the Mariposa courthouse. There are many architecturally, historically interesting, buildings in town. Also, a stunning example of one of the largest and most refined pieces of crystallized gold in existence is the "Fricot Nugget," which is presently housed in Mariposa's California Mining and Mineral Museum. Mariposa is located in a most idyllic setting, surrounded by oaks, pine trees, chaparral, and impressive hills. The only all-year-round access to Yosemite National Park is by way of Mariposa. Of great renown is Mariposa's own "Talking Grizzly Bear." (It's amazing what a little fiberglass, and recording tape, can accomplish).

Jennifer Tipp's Story

I've lived in Mariposa since I was two months old. My parents and family are well known in Mariposa. We've all played a role in the town's development over the years. My sister is a school teacher and two of my brothers own their own businesses; one in Mariposa and the other in the neighboring town of Oakhurst. My uncle was a retired construction supervisor for the state, and before his death six years ago, helped with the construction of the town's sewer system. He was always proud of that project. My story happened to me when I was growing up in my grandmother's house. Before moving to Mariposa, my family lived in Merced, a larger town about 30 miles west of Mariposa. My parents were having a difficult time making ends meet when I was born. They were a young, married couple in their 20s, and already had a large family consisting of my two older brothers. My sister was soon to follow me within two years. As I said before, just two months after I was born, my family moved into my grandparent's house in Mariposa. Fortunately, my grandparents owned two houses. We moved into the larger one with the basement, while my grandparents stayed in the smaller one. The larger house needed repairing—the walls, a totally new kitchen, the plumbing, and some electrical work. Both my father and grandfather immediately got into remodeling what was needed, and before long the house was livable. As I grew older, my parents told me the stories of all the work it had taken to complete this process. I also remember how wonderful it was growing up among all the tall trees in the yard. It was great!

My grandmother was a wonderful baker, and I recall clearly the fresh, wild, blackberry pies she'd make from scratch. She'd gather the berries off the vines that were growing wild all around the property in the summer time, and both she and my mother would spend hours kneading dough and baking pies. I know this took a lot of work, but people loved those pies enough to pay a good price for them. My brothers and I would sit outside using large rocks as chairs, each with a coffee can full of berries. We would eat so many berries that before long, we'd have a case of the runs. Looking back, I'd have to say that was a small price to pay for such a feast.

Well, about my ghost story. When I was about nine, I remember how much fun I'd have going down into the basement of the house and playing with my dolls. I had the usual little girl doll tea parties, where I dressed the family cat like a baby, which he hated. But one afternoon, something very strange happened to me. I had spotted a mouse scurrying along the basement

floor. I was so excited. I thought that the mouse was so cute. Immediately I imagined catching it, placing it in a box, and keeping it as a pet. I ran after it, lifting boxes, and searching among the cast-off trash for the mouse. Looking back now, I am aware that the mouse could have bitten me, but at the time I didn't seem to care.

As I turned over a dusty blanket that was covering a box, I spotted a small photo. The photo was of a young woman in a white dress with a large bow in her hair. It was framed in a beautiful wood frame that had carvings of small oak leaves and acorns. I was mesmerized by it. The face of the woman was so lovely, and at the same time she seemed to look directly at me

*"I spotted a small photo
of a young woman."*

with those dark eyes of hers. Remember, I was only nine years old at the time. Her dress was very pretty, and it closely resembled a dress that a doll of mine had. As I said earlier, I was spellbound by her photo, and she appeared very striking to me.

I carried the photo to the foot of the stairs and leaned it against the wall. I returned to continue looking for the mouse. Among the other forgotten items scattered about the basement I found a pair of small, women's, old black shoes with ribbons, a torn, stuffed monkey with yellow, glass eyes, and lots of old clothes that smelled of mold.

I decided to show the photo to my grandmother, and ask her if she knew who the woman was. Seeing it, my grandmother told me the woman was beautiful, but was unknown to her. She

"I found a torn, stuffed monkey with yellow, glass eyes."

said she didn't know anything about the photo or its history, and that I should ask my grandfather. Then she ordered me to, "Take that old, musty, dusty picture out of the house. It smells terrible."

After taking it outdoors, I took a rag and wiped off the years of dirt and dust from the glass. I wanted to hang it on my bedroom wall. I asked grandfather about it but he didn't have a clue as to how it got in the basement. He said, "I haven't had the time to look at every corner of this property. It must have belonged to one of the previous owners." I remember my mother saying, "That woman's eyes are scary. If you want to hang that thing up on your wall, I don't want you having nightmares." I promised her that I would not have nightmares, and soon the picture was hanging above my dresser. I decided to give the woman a name. While I was flipping through a seed- supply magazine that grandmother had on her kitchen table one day, I spotted a picture of a herb plant named Verbena. I decided that this was going to be the woman's name. It sounded so perfect for her. Every time I passed the portrait, I would say, "Hi, Verbena. See you later Verbena. Good morning, Verbena," etcetera. Nothing strange took place, I didn't see a ghost, or scary things for several months. But one day in my bedroom, as I was drawing in my coloring book, I felt the sensation that someone was in the room with me. Out of the blue I had the impression that someone was standing next to me. I turned, but didn't see anything unusual. But the feeling was so strong that I

"My hairbrush was spinning slowly in a circle!"

stood up and walked to the door. There was nothing out of place. So I turned around and walked toward my bedroom window. Then I noticed that the hairbrush on top of my dresser was spinning slowly in a circle!

Strangely, this didn't scare me at all. I just stood staring at the brush as it spun around. Directly above the dresser was Verbena's photo. I looked at Verbena's dark eyes and said, "Verbena, are you doing this to my brush?" As soon as I had said this, the brush stopped spinning. I knew Verbena was making the brush move. I know I had a wild imagination as a young girl, but I also knew this was not something I had imagined. Again, I spoke, "Verbena, if you play with me, I promise not to tell my mother about you, okay?" There was no answer to my request, and when the hairbrush no longer moved, I decided to continue coloring in my book. I soon forgot the whole incident.

After dinner that evening, I took my crayons and went for a walk to an open field behind our house. The day before, beneath two oak trees, my brothers and I had built a house out of two large cardboard boxes. I wanted to make the boxes look more like a house, so with my favorite can of crayons I was going to draw some curtains on the outside of the boxes. Here's when strange things started to happen. As I was walking to the

field, suddenly I felt two hands grab my waist and lift me into the air! I wasn't lifted very high, just lifted high enough so that I couldn't feel the earth beneath me. It was a wonderful feeling. You can't imagine how exciting this feeling is for a nine year old to actually feel like flying! It was great. My legs simply dangled as I was carried over the grass. I was carried for just a few yards, then I was gently released. Because of the experience I had had with the hairbrush, I immediately knew that Verbena was behind this. I was full of mixed thoughts. I knew this was not normal, but at the same time I was not scared. It was fun, and I wanted more. "Verbena please do me again, please, please," I said. The spirit once more lifted me into the air and let me down. It was thrilling!

After that, Verbena would lift me on command. I never did this in anyone's presence, or told anyone. I wanted it to be my secret. Something that really concerned me was that if I asked to be lifted too many times, I might scare the ghost, or drive her away forever. That was the very last thing I ever wanted to have happen. I didn't even tell my mother. But I always made sure to say, "Thank you, Verbena" after each play session we had. I also used to bring her flowers and pretty rocks that I would find. These "little treasures" I would place on top of my dresser, under her photo. Mother never suspected a thing. But one day I came very close to being discovered. As I was standing next to the washing machine, I asked Verbena to lift me up. As usual I was slowly lifted about a foot off the floor. Suddenly, while I was up in the air, I heard my mother's footsteps approaching the door. I panicked and Verbena must have noticed this because I was quickly dropped to the floor! Luckily, my mother didn't see anything. This incident scared me so much that I didn't ask to be lifted for several days afterwards. As time went

by, I got involved with friends and school activities. I also started to spend less time at home at the end of the school day. I'd go to friends' houses and attend several social activities that occupied most of my attention. Being lifted up in the air became less and less exciting for me. One evening I decided to remove Verbena's photo from my room. I asked my mother if she would mind if I hung it on the living room wall. Mother didn't seem to care any longer, and I guess she had grown to like the photo after all. She said, "Go ahead, just don't make any big, unnecessary holes on my walls." A few minutes later, Verbena's photo was hanging in the living room, and on the wall where her photo used to hang, I now had a poster of my teen idol, Donny Osmond. It didn't take long for Verbena to demonstrate her displeasure at this change. No matter what type of tape, push pins, or glue I used, Donny's poster would curl at the edges, and the pins would pop out of the wall. Before the end of the day, Donny would be on the floor. I definitely knew that Verbena was behind this activity. No one in my family had admitted touching it. Verbena had made her displeasure known and the message was clear. She wanted her picture to be placed back in my room. I felt personally attacked by this, because I had kept my half of the bargain—not telling anyone of our secret for over a year. And now she was throwing my poster to the floor and doing things to punish me. Maybe it was due to my adolescent age, but I became defiant and stubborn. I thought that if she could be rude to me, then I could be just as rude to her. I took her photo off the living room wall and walked down to the basement. I hung it on the wall next to my father's work table. I said out loud, "Verbena, I don't want to play with you anymore." Then I turned, and walked up the stairs to my room. That night, before going to bed, I experienced a woman's voice in my room that spoke the word, "No." The word "No" is all she said. I knew this had to be Verbena speaking to me. I had never had a ghost experience like that before. I knew it was Verbena voicing her displeasure at being returned to the basement once again. But as I said before, I was a stubborn kid. I answered, "Verbena, I don't want to play anymore, so leave me alone." I guess I made my intentions very clear because I never head her voice again. Since that time I have not been visited by Verbena. Many years have now past, and about the only thing unusual, or ghostly, that I have witnessed since then, has been a sensitivity to entering strange houses or buildings. An example of this is when I might be invited to someone's home. As I enter the house, I'll receive a strong feeling of trouble, anger, or even a shortness of breath. My husband understands that if I give him a look like, "I've got to get out of here," he knows not to argue with me anymore, and we soon make an excuse to leave. I also get strange impressions of people that I only tell my husband about. If we go to a movie or restaurant, or anywhere where a group of people are gathered, I'll begin to focus on one individual and immediately will be able to describe the person's health, and other personal issues. It's weird, but I can do this without even trying.

My eyes will scan the crowd and I'll zero in on someone. Soon there will be a little voice in my head telling me about their problems, etcetera. The scariest part is when I see a dark, misty image of a human form around the person I'm watching. Depending on how closely this image stands to the person, the more uncomfortable I get. Now, all this dark figure does is stand next to the person, but it gives me the impression that something bad will soon take place to him or her. That's scary.

I have two daughters of my own now, and those girls are very aware of their mother's gift. They can't get away with any nonsense, believe me! As for my husband, I love him very much, but he also knows better than to do anything that would cause me to be suspicious. I've got a few "helpers" on the other side, and they like to tell me all they see and hear. He's aware of this and I've never had any problems. If you know what I mean. As for Verbena's photo, I have it hanging in my sewing room. I like looking at it from time to time. I would have liked to have known her as a friend when she lived. I hope she is doing well in her spirit form. I've never wanted to communicate again with her since my childhood. Something tells me it would not be a safe thing to do.

COULTERVILLE

Located on Hwy. 49, at the junction of Hwy. 132, just a few miles north of Mariposa, is the small community of Coulterville. Standing on Main Street with only the light from the crescent moon, it isn't difficult to regress in time and imagine the shadowy figures of a mule-pack train as it might have made its way down Main Street. The town was named after founders George and Margaret Coulter, who opened the first trading and retail shop in the area. Coulterville was initially named Maxwell's Creek, but in the year 1872 the U. S. Postal Service officially changed the name from Maxwell's Creek to Coulterville. The Coulters provided the local miners with much-needed supplies and a trading post all under a round, blue canvas roof. Because of their habit of flying a small Stars-and-Stripes flag from the entrance to their shop, it soon became known as a landmark for travelers, and was given the unofficial name "Banderita," or "little flag," by the Mexican miners. Coulterville was not unlike most small gold rush towns, in that it had its share of disastrous fires. These fires took place at 20-year intervals: 1859, 1879, and 1899. Today, Coulterville is a State Historic Landmark with 47 designated historic buildings and sites, all located within the town limits. Surrounded by rugged and steep terrain, the land is dotted with large native oaks which stand as rugged witnesses and guide posts to the town's history.

MICHAEL MARTINEZ'S STORY

My wife, Juanita, and I settled in Coulterville right after I retired from the Federal Prison system in 1994. I had worked as a Correctional Officer in Lompoc, California, for 15 years. I won't lie to you, working for that facility on a daily basis was very intense and stressful. Although I miss the friendships I made with my co-workers during all those 15 years, I was very glad to leave when I did. I witnessed some terrible things that we as correctional officers have to confront as part of our jobs. Prisoners really don't give a damn about life, or anyone else's life, when they know they have to spend the rest of theirs within a concrete cell. It's pathetically sad.

During the last two years of my employment, I was assigned to work the Special Housing Unit or "SHU." This is an infamous area of the prison that isolates "problem" inmates from the rest of the prison population. Whenever they are taken outside of their cells, for their safety and ours, these inmates are always placed in handcuffs and leg shackles. This unit also maintains a zero-tolerance policy for misbehavior of any kind. The inmates know this, and the policy is enforced to the letter. Given this, we do have the occasional inmate that wants to physically challenge this policy, and this always turns into a "no win" situation for the inmate. Sure, some isolated abuses have taken place, and as we speak, those inmates have law suits pending in the courts, but I'm betting that the conditions at Lompoc are no different than those at other maximum facilities in the United States. After all, these guys are not society's best, by any stretch. My own ghost story took place at the Lompoc facility. Looking back at my experience, it was one hell of a thing to witness. Something I will never, ever forget. Not only did it change me in regards as to how I used to view the afterlife, it also changed my view of evil as being something distant, or relegated to the Bible. I mean to say that if evil wishes to present itself, it can and is, from my experience, ready to do so at anytime. All that is necessary is for a person to allow evil to take over himself willingly. I know that there are individuals who have no problem in welcoming evil to do just that. My experience at Lompoc proved that to me.

I still have reoccurring thoughts, and sometimes, even nightmares about the experience. I know I'll never totally be able to forget what I saw. You need to understand that I've only spoken about this to my wife, and a handful of others who I trust. Although my assigned permanent unit is the Special Housing Unit, my experience that night didn't take place there, but at the Intake Unit. Transferring of prisoners at night is not unusual and is, in fact, preferred by the prison system due to light street and highway traffic, which lessens the possibility of a traffic accident. But more importantly the inmates at the prison are "locked down" for the night, which alleviates the possibility, and obvious disruption that might be caused, by an inmate spotting a fellow gang member, rival, etcetera. Boredom causes stress, and given any reason no matter how small, an inmate will focus all his attention on any miniscule disruption to elevate his daily routine. A very different world exists within a prison's walls. A strange world indeed. My story begins one Friday evening at the Intake Unit. The Intake officers, including myself, were expecting an inmate prison transfer from Terminal Island, Long Beach, California to arrive at 11 p.m. I happened to be covering for an officer who was ill at the time. The necessary paperwork and cell had been prepared ahead of time for the transfer, so we expected that everything would run smoothly. As is policy, our Intake Unit received the phone call advising us that the van had arrived at the prison grounds. Our unit's doors were opened, and the prisoner was escorted out of the van, into the facility, within the Intake area. The prisoner, a middle-aged, white man, was handcuffed and had his ankles in leg chains. As is customary, I and four other officers walked the prisoner to his isolation cell. He was also strip-searched for any contraband. During this phase of the intake, notes are taken to record any scars, or tattoos, that can identify the prisoner. These notes are charted in the intake file and follow the inmate for the rest of his life. I was surprised by the number of tattoos this guy had all over his body. Apparently he belonged to a White Supremacist group, because of the usual insignias and symbols. But this guy also had tattoos that were malevolent. Tattoos of Satan, and numerous other symbols of pentagrams, daggers, skulls with bat wings, and so on. New prisoners with a rap sheet history as brutal as this prisoner's were kept isolated for a few hours or days, before being reassigned to their permanent cell, for reasons too numerous to mention here.

Aside from the inmate's weird body art, the transfer went smoothly. Nothing out of the ordinary took place except for one thing. The hispanic officers who delivered the prisoner kept referring to him as "El Diablo" (The Devil), because of his tattoos. They informed us that this prisoner was a "special" one. After reading his criminal record, "horrible" and "monstrous" are the only two words I can use to describe his heinous history of crime. The inmate was very violent, and if I described any of what was written in his file, I would run the risk of having someone, who might read my story, possibly identify him. I'll just say this: he murdered three family members, not his own, through starvation. That's all I can say for now. Well, after we contained the prisoner in his cell, the officers, me included, walked back to our observation station and settled in for the night. Located at the observation station are video monitors that scan the halls, activity rooms, and bathrooms every few seconds. There are also sensitive microphones that are placed in these areas. This is all state-of-the-art equipment, and very necessary. At 1:10 a.m., we heard a movement coming from one of the halls. Quickly we viewed the monitor and noticed that one of the doors to an inmate's cell was slowly opening! We prepared ourselves for a confrontation and rushed to the cell. As we arrived, we saw that the inmate was asleep in his bed and the door was opened about two feet. We woke up the inmate and asked him to explain the situation. He was totally perplexed, and it was obvious our questioning had caught him by surprise. We "shook down" his cell and clothing and found nothing, no key, or homemade tool. Nothing at all which he could have used to open the door.

Throughout the incident the new inmate "El Diablo," watched and occasionally made snickering noises. At one point he said, "Azrael is walking the halls, boys. Better keep your eyes open. Azrael is making sure you guys treat me with respect." We told the jerk to quiet down and mind his own business. He gave me a stupid smile, turned away, and said nothing more. I rechecked the lock on the door and found it worked fine. We had no explanation for this and couldn't even begin to guess as to why it had opened as it did. Perplexed by what had taken place we made a note in the log book and immediately had a technician attend to the problem. Back at the observation station I could clearly see the technician scratching his head in confusion. He was obviously puzzled by the door. He said, "Can't find a thing, it all checks out fine." At 2:20 a.m. the microphone picked up a noise coming from the same hall. I listened with the other officers and we identified a moaning sound. It is not unusual for inmates to have nightmares, so we listened without much concern. But suddenly the moaning became a series of screams. We turned on the main hall lights and rushed to the cell. We approached the inmate's cell and discovered him standing on his bed in the corner. He told us he had seen a black figure. "I saw the devil, you've got to believe me, I saw the devil standing right there. It was big and black and had a white face!" he said. We told the inmate to be quiet and get over his nightmare.

The next night, before starting my shift, I checked the log book and read that there had been problems with the new inmate speaking to an imaginary person, and yelling out the name "Azrael." "El Diablo" had been advised by the officer on duty to keep quiet. When the inmate refused, he was taken to the isolation cell. He was to remain in isolation for four days and nights. Because the inmate was away in isolation, I didn't expect anymore trouble. But this was not to be.

At a 2 a.m. the microphone picked up footsteps coming from the hall. I quickly looked at the video camera and noticed a gray image in the upper-left corner of the hall, directly in front of El Diablo's cell. The gray image quickly became a large, dark cloud and thinking we had a fire, the officers rushed to the hall. When we got to the hall, there was nothing burning, no smoke, or flames. Then the strangest thing happened; we all felt a very cold chill come over us. It was a cold—a chill to the very bare bones—that I had never before experienced.

Returning to the observation station, we spoke about the incident among ourselves. No one had an explanation. I decided to keep the video monitor and microphone focused on the hall, and every few minutes I'd give it a quick glance. To my surprise I heard the sound of something heavy, the rasping sound of something being dragged across the floor. I looked at the video screen and what I saw paralyzed me! There was a big—and I mean big—shadowy, black figure moving down the hall. Before I had the chance to alert the other officers, it disappeared. I was sure the officers would think I was crazy if I told them what I had seen, so I decided to keep this to myself. I was shaking. This was something weird. Something not normal. I was not imagining it, I had just seen a ghost! The huge size of it was what I remember most, it was enormous! For the remainder of the night, I was torn between having to glance at the screen, or avoid it altogether. This thing really did shake me up. I decided to call to the isolation unit where El Diablo was being kept. I was close to one of the officers who was stationed there, and asked to speak to him directly. When Peter answered the phone, he didn't give me the chance to tell him about my strange incident, instead he immediately asked, "Mike, what can you tell me about the new guy, we've been having some weird shit going on over here?" Peter told me he and another officer were hearing grinding noises and footsteps coming from the new guy's cell. Of course, after investigating, there would be nothing unusual except for El Diablo stating, "Azrael is walking, boys. He's walking the halls." I didn't add much to what Peter had said, except that I mentioned we were experiencing the same things in our unit. I didn't want to even suggest that I had seen a ghost. The warden would have thrown me out of my chair and into the psych ward for sure! I can't say that I would have blamed him. If nothing else, my short conversation with Peter did give me the comfort to know I was not going totally crazy. It had now been confirmed to me that the paranormal activity was definitely associated with the new inmate. I was feeling uncomfortable knowing that in just one day, the inmate would once more be returning to my unit. My anxiety was growing when I thought of what other manifestations

I might experience. Given everything, this murderer was no ordinary criminal. He had done some horrendous things. Bloody, evil things to his victims. The next night, prior to starting my shift, I was anticipating the worst. When I arrived at the unit I was told that the inmate would not be returning to our unit because he had been transferred to the Medical Unit, and upon his release, he would be transferred to the Special Psychological Unit for evaluation. Apparently he had gone "over the edge" the night before. He was observed tearing and swallowing pieces of his bed sheet, to the extent that he had swallowed enough fabric to cause a gastric impaction that required surgery. No problem, I thought to myself, the bastard would do us all some good if he were to die. A couple of weeks after the inmate had been sent to the Special Psychological Unit, he was transferred to another state, to stand trial for the murder of two children. I decided not to follow up with his case after that. I was just grateful to know that he, and his "Azrael" ghost, had been sent far away from Lompoc. I know that many people do sincerely believe in such things as ghosts and the paranormal. I admit that I was never one of those types, until I myself experienced such a thing. Today, I'm not the same person. I used to think all that talk about ghosts was for "kooks." I've changed my thoughts about that. That black thing I saw walking the hall convinced me that such things do exist. Evil really does live in the hearts of men, and I've seen it literally walk! Would I welcome another experience like that again? No way, no way!

A HISTORICAL NOTE

Azrael is the name given to the Angel of Death in the Judeo-Christian-Islamic world. The name is of Hebrew derivation, and its literal meaning is "whom God helps."Islamic teachings describe that, "When the angels Michael, Gabriel and Israfel failed to provide seven handfuls of earth for the creation of Adam, the fourth angel on this mission, Azrael, succeeded, and because of this feat, Azrael was appointed to separate body from soul." The Koran also states that Azrael was given "all of the powers of the heavens to enable him to master death." Further, "When a righteous person dies, Azrael comes with a host of divinity, carrying sweet odors of paradise and makes the soul leave the body like a drop taken out of a bucket of water. Though, when a wicked person dies, Azrael comes in the company of demons, who pull the soul out as with iron spits." In Jewish literature, it is written that "when the soul sees Azrael, it 'falls in love', and thus is withdrawn from the body as if by a seduction."

COLUMBIA

Columbia is a rich gold town that has become a living history museum. Columbia State Historic Park started life in 1859 as a commercial hub for the area's miners. Today, Columbia State Historic Park is an educational, sightseeing attraction for people from all over the world. It is also a vital, living community for those who live in, and around, it. The original buildings with their iron doors from the 1840s have been restored to house businesses in keeping with the historic theme of the park. Approximately 96 percent of the buildings are original. In 1860 a fire destroyed several of the buildings; they were replaced within the year. The town was accepted as a state park in 1945 at the urging of area residents who wanted to preserve the Mother Lode's most intact gold rush town. The history of Columbia is rich in gold. According to most reports, the first miners arrived here in 1850. Dr. Thaddeus Hildreth, his brother George, and a handful of other miners found gold while camped near today's main parking lot. Another report states that a group of Mexicans

panned for gold at the same spot in relative secrecy for four or five months prior to the Hildreth party happening upon them. Within a month, about 6,000 miners lived in a tent and shanty town called Hildreth's Diggings. The name was changed to American Camp, then to Columbia, in 1850. By the end of 1852, the new town had more than 150 stores, saloons, other businesses, a Sunday school, Masonic lodge, and a branch of the Sons of Temperance. In addition to being a state park, Columbia has been the setting for many movies, television shows, and commercials.

MARIA B. FULLER'S STORY

I'm originally from Livermore, California. As of today I've been employed at the park for about five months. My position is Park Aid. Primarily, I'm a maintenance worker, and when necessary, I assist the public with interpreting certain exhibits and answering their questions.

My first weird experience at Columbia took place just two months ago, at the Fallon Theatre. A girlfriend of mine was paying me a visit me one evening, and before we both realized it, aside from it getting way too late for her to make her drive back home, when she got into her car it wouldn't start. We took our turn attempting to get the car's ignition to turn over, but having no success, I convinced her to spend the night at the theatre. At the time, the theatre was empty of any other persons, so it was not an inconvenience to the staff for her to spend the night. After I left her, she settled down for the night, and was in good spirits. But at about 2 a.m. that night, I received a call from her, complaining that she was frightened by all the noises, and footsteps she was hearing. I thought this was very strange because I knew that the theatre was empty, but because of the nervous tone in her voice, I got into my car and drove to the theatre to comfort her. As we sat on the theatre's stage talking, she started to describe the noises to me. Suddenly, I felt the weirdest feeling come over me. I began to feel the sensation of someone, a ghost, brushing against me. It was a sensation that I can only describe as being similar to that of

Fallon House Theatre

brushing up against a large, heavy, object such as a curtain. I instantly knew that the two of us were not alone. This was not normal, I thought to myself. Not wanting to scare my friend, I held my breath, and rubbed my arms. I looked all around the room and saw nothing.

My friend knew by my strange behavior and the look on my face that something was not right. Before she had the opportunity to speak a word, she and I both fell silent. We "felt" that something was about to take place, and not knowing what, we simply waited, not moving a finger. Then a movement in the balcony caught my eye. I turned my head and glanced up at the balcony, and I saw the figure of a woman! She was standing, directly facing in my direction. Instinctively, I knew she had appeared for

"I saw the figure of a woman!"

me to see her. I was unable to make out any details of her dress, because she appeared to be made of ice—clear, yet with form. Her eyes, her whole face, was just a big smear, as if they had been rubbed completely off! I just stared at this figure, and watched as she turned, took a few steps, and disappeared! I was in shock. I didn't want to discuss the feelings we both had after that. All I want to say is that it was quite a shock for us both. A few days later, I spoke to some employees at the park about my experience. They informed me of a well-known story regarding a fire that had killed a woman at the theatre many years ago. This woman had become trapped in the theatre, between the buildings that currently are the ice-cream parlor and the hotel. Historically, it has been documented that there were three major fires that had consumed a lot of old Columbia in the years 1852, 1857, and 1922. The unfortunate woman had burned to death in one of these fires. Columbia was a heavily populated town. At one time it had over 6,000 inhabitants. I imagine there must have been a lot of personal loss during every one of these historic fires. Was the spirit of the faceless woman I had spotted at the theatre that of the burned woman? I tend to think so. And what about the spirit that brushed against me, and the footsteps my girlfriend heard? Were they all connected to the tragic fire, perhaps? Since that night I haven't had another ghost experience at the theatre. But as you know, I've only been working at the park for just a few months. There's still a lot of opportunity for other things to take place.

About the only other strange example that comes close to what I experienced at the theatre is the feeling I get some nights when I walk alone in the park. Just a few storefronts from the theatre is a group of trees. When I walk past these trees, I get the strongest, eeriest feeling that someone is watching me from among them. I'm usually very comfortable walking through the park at night, alone. I can stroll anywhere in the park and feel totally comfortable, but the one area that makes my skin crawl is the one with these particular trees. It's difficult to explain, but I swear I can hear the projection of anger. The angry voice of someone saying, "Don't you come near here," or "Get away from here!" I get the impression that something very negative took place at this spot. Right where those trees now grow. I can't explain it, but I just feel it.

"I feel that someone is watching me."

PARK RANGER LOGAN TEJON'S STORY

My story took place more than 16 years ago. At that time I was employed by the California State Park Service. I'm a Native American from the Tule River Indian Reservation, just west of the town of Porterville. My mother, who worked for the tribal office, informed me of a job announcement that the tribal office had received through the mail. The job was for a park ranger at the historic village of Columbia. I fit all the required criteria for the position and, after submitting my application, I was hired a few months later. After I had found a small house in the nearby town, I soon started my new job at the park. My position was Historic Interpreter. Like everyone else who was employed at Columbia State Park, our positions did not just limit us to function within our professional title. We were required to understand other obligations at the park. This usually meant that we "crossed over" to other job descriptions when necessary. For example, I might be asked to lead a tour during the day, then do security watch the following night, etcetera. On a few occasions I would substitute in other areas of the park when an employee called in sick, or missed a day or two. My ghost experience at the park took place one early evening as I was taking a group of tourist on an interpretive walk. I had no idea that within a span of a few hours, my outlook on the paranormal would change as a result of that tour. Toward the end of the tour, one member of the group who was about thirty something asked me, "Excuse me, but do you know if the park is haunted?" I answered, in as much of a professional manner as I could, "Well, that's a common question. Due to the antique look of the buildings, and the town's exceptionally rich history, I can see how some people might associate it with ghosts." I also informed the woman that I personally had never had any type of encounter with a ghost at the park. However by her negative facial reaction, I could tell she was not convinced in the least by my answers. When I informed the group that the tour would be ending in just a few minutes, the same woman and her boyfriend both came forward and asked me if I could spare a few minutes alone with them, so they could describe a ghost experience they had recently had at that park. I told them that would not be a problem. And at the end of the tour, we three sat at a bench under a tree where they proceeded to tell me their story: "Last night at about 9 p.m. my boyfriend and I were walking through the park when we both spotted the ghost of a small man standing next to one of the doorways. He was dressed in dark clothing, and as we walked past him, he simply stared at us, not giving us a wave of his hand, or any courteous gesture."

Caught off guard by her story, I asked her what had made her think this man was a ghost? She said, "As we walked past him, we noticed that his face was very pale and had distinct dark outlines. This gave us a creepy, scary feeling." The boyfriend continued by saying that he had said, "Let's stop across the street and watch what he does." She said, "We acted as if we were tired from walking, and sat down on one of the public benches. We were only about 50 feet away from the man, so even though it was dark, we easily had a clear view of him." The boyfriend then said, "The man might be a tourist acting out the fantasy of playing a ghost and scaring people, or he might even be employed with the park service." The woman continued

"He simply stared at us."

the story by telling me they had both watched the man for about five minutes until she had had enough, and had told her boyfriend the ghost was scaring her. The ghost man was still as could be, staring straight ahead, and this was freaking her out. She said, "My boyfriend saw how this was affecting me and spoke to the man, saying 'Hey, what's up!' At that, the ghost man slowly turned away from us, and seemed to float towards the doorway of the building directly behind where he had been standing. As he reached the door he disappeared in the darkness! We both were amazed and puzzled. We cautiously walked over to the building, and looked through the door's window. It was dark, except for the dim light of a small adjacent room. We turned the door knob, but it was locked. As I said, we followed this man

immediately after he disappeared from us. He did not have enough time to place a key into the door, open it, and enter without us watching him. And for God's sakes, he floated across the ground!" I attempted to explain to the couple that as far as I was aware, the park service did not employ actors to play the role of ghosts, especially after closing hours. They were not convinced, and urged me to ask the superintendent about their experience. I assured the woman that I would try and find out who was behind this. They both were so concerned with what they saw, that she gave me her home phone number and address so I could let them know the outcome of my investigation. The next day I asked several employees and no one knew anything about any employees or actors dressing up and portraying ghosts. I filed a report with the supervisor, and left it up to her to do the remainder of the follow-up investigation.

Some months after this incident, a film crew had scheduled to shoot some footage in Columbia. Not only does Hollywood love the location of Columbia, but film companies from other areas of the world also feel its unique attraction. Columbia's old buildings give off a very historic and authentic aura of the Old West, because we get film crews into the park many times throughout the year. This time, the film company that was scheduled to come into the park had traveled from London. The crew arrived without incident, and began setting up their trailers and positioning their lights. I was employed to provide the necessary security for the set, and was also hired by the film crew to take the film staff around the park and nearby town. I guided them to the local restaurants, historic sites, etcetera. One staff crew member searching for the best locations to film was in charge of operating a mobile camera unit. I accompanied him as he set up his camera and actors at different locations throughout the park. His shots were taken in buildings, under porches, on top of buildings, and generally throughout the park. At the end of the day he and I met to discuss the shooting schedule, for the following day. The purpose being to shoot around, and not to disrupt, the flow of visiting tourists.

I remained with him as he entered a movie trailer filled with the company's editing equipment. After he took a quick review of what he had filmed that day, he seemed strangely baffled by what he had seen on the film. He rewound the video and appeared just as perplexed. He asked me to take a look at the video screen. We both spotted a strange person who appeared in one of the shots, who was not part of the acting crew. He asked me if I knew who this individual was, or if he was employed with the park service. He re-ran the video for me, and sure enough there appeared a small man dressed in a dark hat and clothing, standing by one of the old buildings. The video caught this strange man as he stood by the building, turned, and walked towards a very old, large tree. He again turned to his left, then "disappeared" by a doorway. He didn't just walk into the doorway and enter the building, he "disappeared" under the doorway. I had no idea who this person was, but I immediately recalled the story the couple on my tour had described to me about the ghost they had seen, just two months before. I got a chill, and asked the cameraman if this man had appeared in other shots. He said this was the only one, then said, "Logan, if I didn't film this myself, I would have thought this guy was staged, but I think we've captured a ghost on film." I was surprised. I could only respond with a nervous, "Wow!"

Once word got around about the ghost on the video, other park staff eagerly asked to view it. One female employee

"He turned left then disappeared."

related to me in confidence, that she had never seen the ghostly man, but she had had her own experience with voices in that same building. She said she had not told anyone about her story, because she hoped the memory of it would leave her in time. But after viewing the film, she decided to describe to me what happened to her one afternoon: "At about 6:30 one evening, I entered the store to check on a light bulb I had noticed had been left on. When I walked to the rear of the store, I immediately felt the presence of someone in the room with me. This was strange, because I knew I was alone, and I didn't hear footsteps, or the door open behind me.

There was enough sunlight entering from the windows, so I was not at all in a darkened room. As you know, Logan, the room is also not very large, so I could obviously tell if I were alone or not. The strange feeling that someone was standing right next to me was very strong. I turned around and faced the front windows. I said, 'Anyone here?'

Suddenly, I clearly heard a male voice state the words, 'Women don't belong here, women don't belong here!' I froze in place and said, 'Who's there, who's there?' I kept still. Without warning, I felt the the pressure of a cold hand being placed at the area between my shoulder blades. That was enough. I shot out of that room like a bullet! I've not told anyone about this experience before. But since that day, every time I pass that store, I turn away not wanting to see what might be glaring back at me from the inside the window."

As for myself, I've not had any further contact with the cameraman, or his crew, from London. And aside from these incidents, I've not heard of any other ghostly activities that have taken place at Columbia. There must be others who have had something strange happen to them at the park. Given the large number of tourists who visit Columbia each year, I wouldn't be surprised if there exist photographs with images of ghosts, that just happened to have been captured on film. As I said earlier, I haven't worked at Columbia for over 16 years. A lot can happen in 16 years. The ghost man must have appeared to someone within this time.

REDDING

The city of Redding is located in Shasta County, which in turn lies at the heart of the eight-county Shasta Cascade region. Within this county there are numerous natural treasures including Shasta Lake, Lassen Volcanic National Park, four state parks, Lake Shasta Caverns, and numerous other sites of splendor. The Sacramento River also meanders its way through the city of Redding, offering opportunities to view various species of waterfowl. Redding was named after the first land agent for the California and Oregon Railroad, Benjamin B. Redding. In the year 1872, the town was bounded by North, South, East and West Streets. In 1872, the post office was established, and the city was incorporated in 1887. Redding has been the county seat of Shasta County since 1888.

SHARI TURNER'S STORY

I'm the manager of Aaron Brothers store #218. I've been working at the store since it opened in January 2000. Although I enjoy my job, my employees and I have noticed a recurring pattern of strange "goings-on" that have started to gnaw at our senses. Not only have I personally witnessed a spirit in the store, but some of the employees have also witnessed unusually bizarre ghostly activity. Unexplainable things will happen in the back, or the front, of the store, whether we are working alone, or not.

My first ghostly experience took place in the month of February, just one month after the store had its grand opening. I was in the showroom stocking the shelves with a recent delivery of 8 by 10 picture frames. The time was somewhere between 7 and 8 p.m. Each shelf unit, or display kiosk, in the store has three levels of shelves. I was stocking one of these kiosks when I heard the crashing noise of many frames falling to the floor. I turned my head in the direction of the noise, and noticed that the frames were not just falling to the floor, but were actually being tossed off the shelves. It was as if an invisible hand was having a great

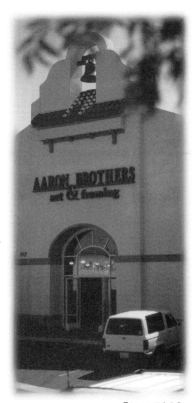

Store #218

time, flinging them off the shelves, one by one, causing a domino effect. I stood there, amazed at what was taking place right before me. Was this really happening, or was I imagining things? I didn't move a muscle. I just stood in place, in total shock, witnessing this weird event. Soon the noise of other frames being knocked over, in other areas of the store, started up. Other store employees who were present at the time also witnessed, and watched, as this strange incident continued. We had no explanation for this, and we chose to simply brush it off as being something that could be easily explained, although I had no explanation. At other times, I've also watched an unusual pattern take place when parents with small children enter the store. The children will automatically be drawn to the store's center kiosk where lots of colorful frames are displayed, and ghost activities have taken place there. This pattern started one day with a mother and child. One day, a mother and her little girl came into the store. The girl walked right up to the center kiosk, and sat herself down on the floor, carrying on a conversation with an invisible child. I watched as the girl talked, and talked to someone whom I couldn't see. The girl would reach over, pick up a frame, hold it up for her invisible friend to see, then place it back on the shelf. This continued until the mother decided to leave. Another time, I watched as a child's picture frame, one that is decorated with animal designs, actually rose up from the kiosk, and projected itself through the air, then landed on the floor, just a few inches from where the employees were working. It was as though the ghost intended for the frame to hit them. Trying not to be visibly scared, we joked that the ghost was just playing with us. To this day, some employees dislike going anywhere near that kiosk. Another time, in the morning when I entered the store, I discovered that the shelves, on which were displayed small paint tubes and two-ounce pots of paint, were in total disarray. This was very strange because the night before, I personally had made sure to straighten up this particular section of the store. The pastel paints had been moved over to the glossy paint section, and the glossies moved over to the pastels. Having the keys to all the doors, and checking all the possible modes of entry, I was positive that no one had entered the store. Again, I attempted to make a joke, to jest about everything that had, and was, continuing to take place, but try as I might, I was at a loss. Even now, I get goose bumps thinking about what took place there. Last winter, during the month of November, I again experienced something. This particular experience was an actual visit from a spirit. It was during the evening hours and I was alone, emptying each of the store's small trash cans into a larger plastic bag, which I dragged behind me. I was doing some general housekeeping, going down each aisle picking up any bit of paper I might spot on the floor. Suddenly, I stopped what I was doing, because I felt the presence of someone's eyes watching me. I mentally told myself that my mind was playing a trick on me, but because of the power of this feeling, I was really freaking out. I tried to overcome this scary feeling, and I kept trying to reassure myself that there was absolutely no other person in the store with me. This feeling became stronger and stronger, so much so that I froze. Suddenly, from down the aisle, I saw something move. I turned my head, and I saw the shadow of a small person dodge away. Immediately goose bumps covered my body. And I wasted no time in leaving the store, and calling it a night. Three nights after this last experience, and again when the store was closed for the day, I was in my office, doing paperwork. The only difference was that this evening I was not alone. An employee was framing artwork in the back room. At one point, I decided to leave my office, and walk through the store to check on the employee. As I made my way through the store, I suddenly spotted a small blonde-haired girl standing next to a kiosk, with her back facing me. I immediately wondered what this child was doing in the closed store. Having taken a good look at the image, to this day I can clearly describe her in detail. She wore khaki shorts, with long white socks, tennis shoes, and a hooded sweatshirt. Her clothing was in the style of the 40s or 50s. Not of the Victorian era, or of an old-fashioned type, but somewhat modern looking. Of course, kids don't dress like that today with the knee socks, so she was definitely from another era. She was also about the age of nine or ten, not frail, but stocky, and a little over four feet tall. Alarmed, I thought that an employee had mistakenly locked this child in the store. I started walking toward this little girl with my arm extended, saying, "Oh hon', I'm sorry, the store is closed and we locked you in." As I got within 10 feet of her she disappeared. She just disappeared! For some reason, the names Abigail and Samantha flashed in my mind.

I don't know why, they just did. Also, as I said, her image was not fuzzy, or wavy. She was clear and very real. As real as any living person. Even stranger was the smell of "child." I don't know how I can relate this scent to you, but she left the lingering smell of a child with me. I felt like running to my fellow employee, and screaming out what I had just seen. But, not wanting her to think I was losing my mind, I kept the experience to myself. To be sure, I was frightened, but because it was the ghost of a little girl, and not an adult, I felt to some degree a little more at ease. Today, I'm more comfortable discussing her apparition with others. I guess time has helped me overcome this. But most important is that I also now have a reason that might explain the unusual mischief that had taken place throughout the store. I believe this little ghost girl was the cause of all that mischief. You might think that that would be the end of my experiences at the store, but just three nights after that incident, another one took place. I was standing at the back of the store, behind the custom-frame counter. The assistant manager was straightening out some portfolios on a shelf. Suddenly, the middle shelf containing all the portfolios that we had both just straightened, were lifted up off the shelf and thrown to the floor! We were stunned and speechless. We quietly picked up the portfolios and went about our day. Still other strange, but common, occurrences are the voices that are heard throughout the store. I'll hear voices, or conversations, going on in different areas. I'll stop what I'm doing, then walk cautiously over to where I heard the voices. As I try to make sense of what is being said, the more I try the less I understand. I can stand right in the actual spot of the voices, but I can't understand the words being spoken. I've even gone outside and walked over to the store that shares a thick cement wall with ours, attempting to see if anyone is still working at that late hour, or playing the radio, I'll look through the dark windows. I've never seen anyone in the closed store. Another employee, Terri, who has also heard the same voices,

"The teddy bear flew off the shelf!"

decided to investigate on her own. She asked several local people if they had any information regarding the history of the land upon which the store was built. Terri called her aunt, who is well acquainted with the area, and her aunt told her that there used to be a large barn on the site. But if there are any deaths associated with the barn, no one has come forward and told me.

Another employee, Lisa, was standing at the counter a few feet away from the kiosk where the activity seems to happen most. There is a teddy bear that is positioned within a shadow-box frame, that sits on a high shelf over 10 feet away from this kiosk. While Lisa and I were helping a customer one night, the framed teddy bear suddenly flew off the shelf, traveled through the air, and landed with a crash, about six inches from Lisa! The frame is not very light. It would have to be picked up with a lot of force to be thrown in this manner. Lisa was obviously not happy with that incident. She could have been seriously hurt. There are no cold spots in the store that are usually connected with spirits, but several workers definitely feel the little girl's spirit. Personally, when I start to feel her presence, I speak out, and say "Okay Abby, tonight let's just have a nice night." I also get the feeling that she doesn't like a lot of clutter, or things to be moved around. I get these impressions because of her practice of tossing frames and clearing off shelves. These are, of course, just the impressions that I get, but as I have already said, my staff and I have actually stood by, watching helplessly, as she's done her "house work." To this day, especially during the winter months, I still see the movement of shadows throughout the store. As soon as fall gives way to winter, I know that things will once again begin to start up. Thankfully, no one has been physically attacked by her, but she has come close to doing some physical harm to Lisa. Look at my arms, I'm getting goose bumps again; all over again just thinking about her.

LISA R. HOWLE'S STORY

I've worked for Aaron Brothers for over a year. My present position at the store is Assistant Sales Associate. I'm aware of there being a presence in the store, because ever since I first set foot inside the building, I've been able to pick up what I call "vibes." And, unusual as it might sound to a nonbeliever, I regularly hear the softly, spoken voice of a young girl. Most recently, the voices of men mumbling in certain areas of the store have become an even more common occurrence for me. I've been told that there used to be an old barn where this store now stands. Shari, our manager, also told me that a local historian had informed her that there was a family who lived on the property, and this family had a young daughter who was killed in the barn. I thought that bit of information was interesting, and might explain some of our ghost's activities. My first experience with this particular child's ghost, who we call "Abby," took place just a month after I began my employment. I recall last October was the month when I began to feel, what I term, my "vibes." This took place during the evening at around 7 p.m., after I had locked all the doors for the night. I was sitting on the floor dusting off frames, at the opposite corner of the kiosk, in the area where our manager, Shari, actually witnessed this little girl's ghost materialize. I was busy dusting the frames when suddenly, directly above me, one of the glass frames came off the shelf, and landed with a loud crash, just a few inches away from me. The frame was shaped in the form of a surfboard, a frame specifically designed for children. I've learned that this ghost, Abby, tends to disrupt and rearrange anything that is associated with children. The surfboard frame was literally picked up and thrown at me. I knew the intention was for it to hit me, I just got that vibe. I was positive that the frame could not have accidently moved itself to the front of the shelf. I had just finished dusting that specific area, and I had moved all the frames on that particular shelf toward the rear. There was no way it could have fallen without help, no way at all. As I said, the kiosk was filled with nothing but colorful children's frames. Since working at the store, I've learned that incidents such as this one are not unusual. They are constantly reoccurring, again and again. I know this might sound strange, but I was more startled than scared. It appeared to me that Abby was trying to get my attention, or perhaps wanted to engage me to play with her in some weird way. Nothing else happened that evening. But, in the weeks since then, if I happen to be standing next to a shelf, or just walking by a kiosk, frames will sometimes be thrown at me. It seems that I'm the chosen one the ghost enjoys reacting to. I mentioned this incident to Shari, and she seemed uncomfortably nervous with the idea of a ghost being in the store. As much as I can tell, she still is, but she's gotten a lot better at dealing with the spirits, and it seems to me, even better at accepting them.

My next experience took place while I was standing in the middle of the store. A whole bunch of frames came flying my way. By chance, Shari was with me, and was a witness to it. Again,

"A framed teddy bear came flying at me!"

this took place in the early evening. There's not much more I can say about this. It's just another example of our little Abby trying to get my attention. But there was another incident that really did shake me. A framed teddy bear came flying at me off a high shelf. This toy teddy was glued within a shadow-box frame, which made it quite heavy. It was unlikely to move on its own because of its weight, or so I thought. It was placed very carefully away from the reach of customers, on a high shelf, behind our framing counter. Because all our displays and supplies are well placed, and secured, we've never had any of these heavy frames move or fall. Well, one day, as I was standing behind the counter, the frame with the teddy bear came off the shelf and broke into pieces right next to me. It missed hitting me by just a few inches. Everyone who witnessed this was very aware that this was not a normal thing to have happened. Oh, well, it must have been Abby doing her tricks once again, I thought. Another time, we got a big delivery of a new product. There were small frames in the shape of kittens, and their arms, tails, and heads were moveable. It was an odd type of frame; a combination of a frame and toy. The legs and arms could be shaped into several positions, and the heads could even be taken off. Needless to say, because they were odd, they were not a big seller for us. We displayed them in the middle kiosk, the one we've since referred to as "Abby's Kiosk." The unusual thing is that for about a month or so, a number of these frames were disappearing from the kiosk. We would discover them tucked away in the strangest spots throughout the store. Some would be up on the highest shelves, in different areas of the store. Behind and between frames, and always with their heads removed. I personally kept my attention on this kiosk for about a week, and didn't notice any children, or adults, fooling around with the frames. At first I was somewhat amused, but then my amusement turned to annoyance and aggravation. I knew that Abby was up to her tricks once again. As I said, I have a continuous feeling at the store. This feeling tells me the ghost of Abby is watching me with her little-girl eyes, and following my every movement as I go about my day. Without any warning, I'll feel an uncomfortable vibration come over me. Abby's presence is a very strong one. And I know that when she seriously wants me to pay attention to her, this vibration gets even stronger. Just a couple of nights ago, at around 9 p.m., again when the store was closed, I had another experience with Abby. I had one of these sensations as I was walking through the store. Soon after, I noticed the movement of a small, shadow-like person following me off to my side. This same incident has now happened twice to me within this very month. I know that Shari gets very uncomfortable when I mention to her that I see shadow images. So I tend to keep these incidents to myself. Also a month ago, I was with another female employee after we'd closed for the day. No one else was in the store and the doors were locked. Soon, we both began to hear voices in conversation. We thought it might be janitors, or someone lingering outside the doors. I looked to see if I could spot anyone, and no one was around. The voices were of two men in conversation. We were unable to make out what was being said, but they were definitely conversing with each other. I've never felt the presence of a male entity or ghost in the building, so this was new and unusual. The voices went on for about a half hour, off and on. Where this will lead to is anyone's guess. To my knowledge, the employees have been the only ones who have witnessed the ghost. Customers have never come to us and said they've seen, or even felt, anything unusual in the store. Even though I do believe ghosts to be true and real, I'm not really scared of Abby, or any other ghosts. They're not a big deal to me. I would like to have the experience of seeing Abby appear to me in total. I think it would be exciting, because I would accept her as being simply the ghost of a child, and nothing more.

SUTTER CREEK

Sutter Creek is a charming, gold-rush town that is located on Hwy. 49, approximately 45 miles from either Stockton or Sacramento. The discovery of quartz gold took place in the area in 1848, and was continuously mined until the mines were shut down by Executive Order in 1942. Founded and named after Captain John Sutter, Sutter Creek had one of the richest "deep rock" mines in the Mother Lode. Gold seekers from around the world came to Sutter Creek in search of quick wealth. The town was incorporated into the county in September of 1854. At the centennial of the first Gold Discovery in 1949, Sutter Creek became a mecca for tourism. Tourism became, and continues to be, a vital part of Sutter Creek's economic foundation. Visitors marvel at the town's gold-rush heritage and its classic Western appearance, which today attracts visitors from around the world. Aside from its prominent Old West–style architecture, examples of the Victorian, New England, and Greek Revival styles are also evident in town. Today, Sutter Creek's main industries, aside from tourism, are lumber and wine. A famous former resident of Sutter Creek is Leland Stanford, founder of Stanford University.

JAY CUSKER'S STORY

My partner and I took the time to carefully choose this house as the best location for our gift shop, which we named Passages. The house had been empty for about 40 years before we occupied it. As of this day we've been operating the business for three years. Before we moved here, our gift shop was elsewhere in town. And before we occupied the house, we had been told that the house had ghosts. Even more surprising was the news that these ghosts were definitely unhappy ones. The primary caretaker, who would regularly clean the house, told us about her own personal experiences with these ghosts. These ghosts caused her to have enough concern for our well-being, so she sat down with us and sincerely recounted her own experiences at the house. She told of one example when she was alone in the house, generally cleaning up the place. Both the mop and broom she had placed against the wall had been picked up into the air and thrown across the room! Immediately after this event, all the doors in the house began to open and slam all around her!

She also informed us that the house was used only occasionally by the owners as a weekend retreat. Eventually, the owners began to use the house less and less until they finally decided to lock it up. The house was built in the 1850s by a sea captain. And when you study the design of the house, you can see it reflects the maritime owner's tastes, because it was built using a ship's blueprint. The porch was built to simulate a ship's deck, and as such, each room of the house opens out onto this "deck." Also, the main, front door entrance leads to a flight of stairs that leads a person to a galley-like, lower level. This sea captain was probably from the East Coast, because there is a very old, large, Eastern Sugar Maple tree growing in the backyard. There are also two other large trees in the front yard, which nurserymen have informed us are either Ash or Elm, and like the Maple, are also native to the East Coast. They've also said that there is a strong possibility that these trees probably don't exist any longer in their native habitat, which is due to such East Coast diseases as Dutch Elm, etcetera.

"We heard there was a spiritual side to the house."

After the captain died, the house was bought by an Italian family, the Brignoli, who had 10 children. The Brignoli family was one of the original families in the Sutter Creek area. I have some old photographs of this family that were taken at the house, on the porch and in the yard. Gus Brignoli, the father, was the last man to have lived and died in the house. He was very well known in the area as a philanthropist of the community. The Brignoli's still own the house, by way of the female lineage. As far as I know, the men never married.

Now, as for ghostly activity, I definitely do feel a presence here in the house, and customers from time to time will describe

The Brignoli women—Christmas Day 1885,
Anita, Molly, Mary, and mother.

Mary Brignoli, "This is the
beautiful woman whose ghost
I've seen."

being followed around the rooms by an unseen person. Customers have said that they have the strong impression of a man that follows them. Customers also have reported catching the tobacco scent of a man's smoldering pipe. I have had my own personal experience with this. Once, as I was talking to two women customers about the ghosts in the house, we were suddenly enveloped in the smell of tobacco smoke. I stared at them and asked, "Do you smell anything strange?" Without hesitation, they knodded, and both responded that they could smell pipe tobacco. I know that there are two ghosts in the house, one a man and the other a woman. I've seen them both, but I see the woman's spirit more often. Interestingly enough, whenever we have sponsored an artist reception, or other such small social gathering at the house, inevitably I'll catch a glimpse of the woman's ghost as she passes by a doorway, or behind one of the party guests. She's always dressed in a long white dress, and again, she only appears when lots of people are gathered in the house. She also likes the nursery room, where I've both seen, and felt, her presence.

Photo taken July 1998 of Susan Ross and immense "ghost orb" on the stairs leading into the front parlor.

Author's note: Ghost orbs are energy, the basic spirit form, the essence of a ghost. These orbs are of an unknown origin that take the form of round globes, or orbs of light, appearing both indoors and outdoors. These energy anomalies usually are present, and at times have been recorded, at sites that are known to have spiritual activity. These orbs can appear randomly in both video and photographic film, and cannot be dismissed as being specks of dust, smoke, flying insects, or electrical static discharge. By virtue of their particular energy, ghost orbs can not be seen by the naked eye. Ghost orbs can change directions very quickly, and it is well known that they react to the presence of people.

I recall when, during our store's grand opening reception, I took a picture of a friend, Susan Ross, as she was walking down

"I definitely do feel a presence here in the house."

the stairs that lead to the parlor. Before taking the picture I began to feel, or sense, the invisible presence of someone standing over me. Undeterred, I went ahead and took Susan's picture, and as you can see from the photo, the resulting image shows a large light, or spirit, appearing on the stairs with Susan. I've been told that these balls of light are called "Ghost Orbs" by parapsychologists, and are explained as being a spirit's energy that is sometimes captured on film.

I've also had other creepy experiences that begin as I go around the house placing new gift items on various shelves. I'll get an "impression" that a ghost might not approve of where I position an item. Suddenly, I'll feel a "heaviness" that will envelop the room I'm in, and I know it will be best if I move the gift items elsewhere. When I do this, the energy in the room will change to become a cheerful and happy one. These days, I'm very sensitive to this. The house, and its unique history, are amazing. My sincere hope is that the ghosts that dwell within it are now as content with it as we happen to be. I believe that the old captain's spirit is also still here, because he must have enjoyed, and loved, his house very much. He must have been very attached to it given all the personal touches he added. He must be very happy with all the attention and positive comments that visitors to the house have made. A Native

American friend of mine, who has visited the house, told me that she "feels" that the captain's spirit is very content with the house in its present state. I would very much enjoy the opportunity to see the sea captain's spirit appear to me. I hope I wouldn't be too scared. But, who knows?

Jamestown

Col. James H. Carson wrote: "On the long flat we found a vast canvas city under the name of Jamestown, which, similar to a bed of mushrooms, had sprung up in a night. A hundred flags were flying from restaurants, taverns, rum mills, and gaming houses . . . the whole presented a similar to that of San Francisco during the winter." Col. James Carson suffered financial losses and left in the summer of 1849. The town slumbered after the gold seekers left for new diggings, but was revived in 1896 when a group of Bostonians purchased the Whiskey Hill Consolidated Gold and Silver Mining Co. They reopened it as the Harvard Mine Sierra Railway in 1897, bringing world commerce to the county.

Everything about Jamestown seemed to slide during the 1920s, after the gold mines had closed, but the town's image began to turn around during the 1970s, when students and business owners began clearing the town and raising funds to

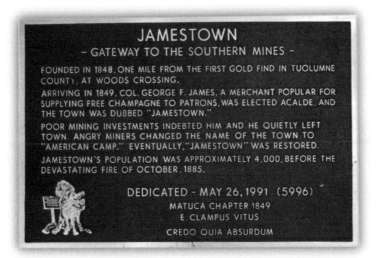

JAMESTOWN
- GATEWAY TO THE SOUTHERN MINES -

FOUNDED IN 1848, ONE MILE FROM THE FIRST GOLD FIND IN TUOLUMNE
COUNTY, AT WOODS CROSSING.
ARRIVING IN 1849, COL. GEORGE F. JAMES, A MERCHANT POPULAR FOR
SUPPLYING FREE CHAMPAGNE TO PATRONS, WAS ELECTED ACALDE. AND
THE TOWN WAS DUBBED "JAMESTOWN."
POOR MINING INVESTMENTS INDEBTED HIM AND HE QUIETLY LEFT
TOWN. ANGRY MINERS CHANGED THE NAME OF THE TOWN TO
"AMERICAN CAMP." EVENTUALLY, "JAMESTOWN" WAS RESTORED.
JAMESTOWN'S POPULATION WAS APPROXIMATELY 4,000, BEFORE THE
DEVASTATING FIRE OF OCTOBER, 1885.

DEDICATED - MAY 26, 1991 (5996)
MATUCA CHAPTER 1849
E. CLAMPUS VITUS
CREDO QUIA ABSURDUM

build a gazebo and park on Main Street. The park has since become a focal point for community events. At the same time the
rest of the historic downtown was revived. Buildings were ren-
ovated in keeping with their original purposes, and many of the
Victorian homes were turned into shops that now feature artwork, gifts, collectibles, and antiques.

THE NATIONAL HOTEL AND SALOON

The authentically restored Historic
National Hotel in Jamestown (one of
the 10 oldest, continuously operated
hotels established in 1859), is filled
with historical reminders of California's gold-rush past. Located in the center of Jamestown, the National Hotel
has played host to travelers for over 140
years. Guests return again and again to
enjoy the National Hotel's quaint ac-
commodations, outstanding cuisine,
and warm and friendly service. Each of

the hotel's nine restored rooms is furnished with wonderful brass beds, regal comforters, lace curtains, and a feeling that lingers from the days when the hotel was in its first glory. Among the newer amenities is modern plumbing with oak pull-chain toilets. All rooms have private bathrooms. Each room is charmingly authentic, individually appointed, and includes most of the original furnishings. The Gold Rush Saloon is furnished with its original 19th-century redwood bar over which thousands of dollars in gold dust was spent. It's not difficult to ponder what it may have felt like to be a gold miner in the 1850s drinking at the bar.

STEPHEN WILLEY

I have been the owner and general manager of the National Saloon since it was opened in 1974. I'm originally from the Monterey Bay area of California. I was born in Salinas and brought up in Watsonville. The hotel is one of the 10 oldest, continuously operated hotels in the state, and it dates back to 1859. As historical records show, the other, older original hotels in the area that were built of wood, caught fire and burned to the ground. In the 1850s, the newer hotels were built of stone. Within the present hotel, we currently operate an upscale restaurant and a full bar. I was not told, or made aware of, any ghost activity on the property when I purchased it. But, immediately after moving in, things started to happen, things that I can only call "unexplained." Reports from visitors, that were noted by employees, described accounts of a woman's spirit wandering the property. Because of these reports, we decided to give the woman's ghost the name "Flo." I've not found any historical records that describe this ghost, and she's never caused any harm, so I can confidently say she's a contented ghost. She also appears to be happy, enjoying her role as a prankster. She's never

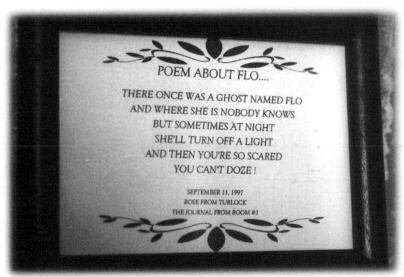

POEM ABOUT FLO....

THERE ONCE WAS A GHOST NAMED FLO
AND WHERE SHE IS NOBODY KNOWS
BUT SOMETIMES AT NIGHT
SHE'LL TURN OFF A LIGHT
AND THEN YOU'RE SO SCARED
YOU CAN'T DOZE !

SEPTEMBER 11, 1997
ROSE FROM TURLOCK
THE JOURNAL FROM ROOM #3

Poem written September 11, 1997, by Rose,
a guest who spent the night in room #3.

been malicious, angry, or scary to those who encountered her. Given this, we all continue to welcome her surprising visits. I myself have encountered her only once, at my home that's attached to, and located directly behind, the hotel. I recall the visit, when I was standing on my porch on a hot summer, breeze-free day. Suspended from the porch were several wind chimes. Suddenly, the largest of the chimes began to vigorously ring. I thought it was odd for only the heaviest, and biggest, of the chimes to start moving. Quite curious, I walked over to the grouping of suspended chimes, and expected to see one of my cats taking "paw-swings" at them. There was no cat in sight. Strangely, as I got directly in front of the tinkling large chime, it immediately stopped ringing. I studied the situation, and found absolutely no cause for this. As I said, there was no wind causing the chime to move as vigorously as it had done. I gave up trying to figure out a reason, turned around, and began to walk into the house. As soon as I had taken a couple steps, surprisingly, the

"Guests report seeing a young woman, in her mid–30s, strikingly pretty, and very self-assured."

chimes started up once more, ringing and moving as if shaken by invisible hands. With a strong sense of resolution in my voice, I spoke loudly, "Flo, stop it!" Immediately, without any further delay, the chimes came to a full, and sudden, stop.

Our employees and guests have had many, many encounters with Flo. Most of these encounters have happened in the hotel. Housekeepers have reported to me that as they have set a stack of clean towels on one side of a bed, they would momentarily turn their backs, and the towels would have been moved to the opposite side of the bed! Other times, when a housekeeper had pulled a shade up, or down, then gone into the next room, upon their return, they'd found the shade in the opposite position. Housekeepers always expect for Flo to move things around. These little "things" happen continually and are expected. Our hotel records report that guests have seen a young woman, in her mid 30s, who is strikingly pretty and dressed in a long, Victorian-style gown. She walks confidently through the dining room, as if she knows where she's headed. She appears to be a very self-assured type ghost. Guest have also reported that their luggage has been picked up and moved to other areas of the room. Also, that the window shades have been pulled in the middle of the night. I've noticed that Flo doesn't make sounds like footsteps, and the scent of perfume that usually accompanies female ghosts has never been associated with Flo. Guest also write personal, short reports about Flo's activities in the hotel room, guest ledgers. Each room has its own ledger, and these books are filled with accounts about Flo.

Flo doesn't seem to favor one room over another, she "hits" them all. But we do have returning guests, who specifically book rooms #3 and #7, because guests say that these rooms have the most activity. But who knows.

We have had very few guests who, out of fear, have canceled a stay at the hotel having heard about Flo. Most guests have a good time knowing that a classy spirit like Flo is watching, making sure they're being treated in the correct, and proper manner she herself had become accustomed to. I'd love to actually have her appear to me. Just so long as she gives me a little warning first. I just enjoy having her around.

"I'd love to actually have her appear to me."

GROVELAND

Groveland has a rich history of being one of the towns that grew up around gold diggings during the California Gold Rush. Although gold brought the area its first rush of people, water also played a major role in the town's fortunes. Today, Groveland serves tourists from all over the world, as well as its more than 7,000 area residents. Originally, Groveland and Big Oak Flat were named Savage's Diggings after James Savage, who discovered gold there in 1848. He left in 1849 when the gold rush started. By 1850, the camp was named Garrotte for its swift and harsh frontier justice. The Golden Rock ditch, from the South Fork of the Tuolumne River, near Hardin Flat, was completed in 1859, ensuring there was enough water for hydraulic mining. By 1860, Garrotte was a boom town. The Big Flat Flume, a link in the ditch, fell with a spectacular crash in 1868. By the 1870s most of the "easy pickings" were gone.

Garrotte became a quiet town catering to cattle ranches and the few tourists who would take the Big Oak Flat Road to Yosemite. The Big Oak Flat Road to Yosemite was unpaved, narrow, and winding. Traffic was one way, and the road was closed during the winter months. In 1875, Ben Savory, owner of what is now the Groveland Hotel, convinced his fellow citizens to rename the town Groveland. In the late 1800s Groveland had a second boom with deep shaft mine and milling operations. The mining boom was over by 1914, but San Francisco had received

congressional approval to build the Hetch Hetchy Water Project. Groveland was selected to be the mountain division construction headquarters, but Groveland received none of the water, so when the project ended, Groveland returned to being the sleepy town it had been before. During World War II, the town was dark and quiet. Everyone was fighting overseas or working in the shipyards. When the war ended, America started building homes. Groveland had another boom, although it was short-lived. Twenty-two small lumber mills were opened, but the lack of water kept the area from growing. Private wells and springs ran dry every summer.

Today, Groveland is a natural stopping spot on Hwy. 120 on the way to Yosemite National Park, and it is a vacation destination in its own right, from which many people take day trips to Yosemite.

GROVELAND HOTEL

The hotel is the largest adobe building in Groveland, and is one of the oldest buildings in the county. Now listed on the National

THE GROVELAND HOTEL
MONTEREY COLONIAL ADOBE
HAS BEEN PLACED ON THE
NATIONAL REGISTER
OF HISTORIC PLACES
BY THE UNITED STATES
DEPARTMENT OF THE INTERIOR
1849

THE GROVELAND HOTEL
QUEEN ANNE REVIVAL
HAS BEEN PLACED ON THE
NATIONAL REGISTER
OF HISTORIC PLACES
BY THE UNITED STATES
DEPARTMENT OF THE INTERIOR
1914

Register of Historic Places, in years past the structure was first used as a trading post, owned and operated by Joshua D. Crippen and Company. The property was later owned and operated as the "Garrote Hotel" by Matthew Foot, a prospector who arrived during the gold rush. In 1857 it became known as the Groveland Hotel.

By 1900, Groveland's economy was driven by the mining industry. The miners' business affairs were carried out at the Groveland Hotel and Bar, a neighboring dance hall, and the nearby saloon. By that time there were at least two other hotels in town, yet the Groveland Hotel was still the largest and most impressive. By 1914, mining had lapsed into an irreversible decline and the second personality of the hotel was "born." The hotel was purchased by Timothy H. Carlon, a successful cattle rancher, who had extensive holdings both inside and outside the county. Timothy Carlon was described as Tuolumne County's first "millionaire cattleman." Walter A. "Peach" Pechart leased the historic hotel from Timothy Carlon and quickly set to work installing games, hiring bartenders, and converting some of the rooms at the back of the hotel into a small "bull pen." Although the Goveland Hotel's bull pen was best remembered for its girls, it was only one of many "sporting houses" in full-steam operation during this period. Present owners, Peggy and Grover

Mosley, took over the hotel in 1990 and in 1992 completed a million-dollar restoration. The hotel today has 17 uniquely decorated rooms, an elegant Victorian dining room and a cozy "saloon." The Mosley's have worked hard to preserve the hotel's historical integrity.

PEGGY A. MOSLEY

Originally I'm from Memphis, Tennessee, and my "claim to fame" is that I was actually a neighbor, and classmate, of rock 'n' roll idol Elvis Presley. Initially I got to California by way of being stationed at the Norton Air Base, in San Bernardino. I spent 13 years in the U. S. Air Force, then upon my discharge, I eventually made my way to Northern California, where in May of 1990, my husband and I purchased the hotel and property. When we came upon the hotel, it was in complete disrepair; the windows were boarded up, and it was in much need of care and money. We really had no idea that under all the dirt, rot, and neglect there was a priceless treasure.

We purchased the property with the goal of restoring and

Humes high school, Memphis, TN. Peggy Simmons (Peggy A. Mosley) Front Row, left to right, seated left of books. Elvis Presley, Back Row, standing at extreme right.

operating it as an historic inn. As the remodeling progressed, we began to get little glimpses of its history. The property also included an original gold mine, located across the creek, in the back of the property. Once we had acquired the property, local folks "opened up" and began mentioning their experiences with the building. An older gentleman in particular, named Ernie Beck, who eight years ago died at the age of 103, told us the history of the property as he knew it, including stories of the ghost. I'll never forget Ernie's words, "Oh, you're gonna' be sorry." Within a short time after moving in, we began to experience really strange things. The remodeling got underway when a group of 19 of our friends came to town specifically to help us with the restoration. During that time, all of us experienced doors in empty rooms being opened and shut, buckets of paint being turned over, spilling paint on the floor, and numerous other unexplainable examples that indicated to us we were not alone. More importantly, we were also told by locals that a gold miner named "Lyle" had lived on the property. Lyle worked the mine on the property, and was known to be a very private man. One day, in 1927, someone noticed after three days that Lyle was missing. Soon he was discovered in his hotel room, dead. Since then, the stories that have circulated tell how Lyle's spirit wanders the hotel. All my employees, past and present, have stories of personal encounters with Lyle's ghost. Lyle's spirit tends to be most active in the winter months. I wish I had a photo of him, so that we could identify his face, with his spirit. I think it would be great to be able to see what he actually looks like. The first significant paranormal thing that my husband and I personally experienced within the building took place during the winter of 1990. My husband was in one room watching television, while I was across the hall in another room, attending to paperwork. My husband came into my room and asked, "Do you hear that? It sounds like the shower in one of the rooms is on." I responded jokingly, "Oh, it's probably Lyle taking a shower." My husband decided to investigate and walked upstairs to the room where the sound was coming from. I watched as he walked down the hall. He got about half way toward the room, when suddenly the sound of the shower stopped. He came flying back, and said, "Did you hear that, the shower stopped!" I said, "Well, I guess Lyle finished his shower." My husband didn't think my answer was very funny. Up to that point he had refused to believe in the existence of ghosts, but I could tell he was quickly becoming a believer. Another weird experience took place one evening, quite late, at about 11:30. The hotel was up and running by then, and we had a group of 18 travel writers, employed by Delta Airlines, who were attending a meeting on the first floor of the hotel's dinning room. Part way through the brief introduction I had been asked to give about the hotel, I touched upon our resident ghost, and things started up. As soon as I mentioned Lyle's name, the lights in the room became dim, then bright, then dim again. A definite invisible presence, and a coldness, were felt by everyone. I could see that each guest was very uncomfortable. People even uttered audible gasps of

"A wooden chair that was placed against the wall, was now against the bed touching her mattress!"

surprise. I ended my introduction with a quick, but courteous, thank you, and exited the room.

One woman guest who had been staying alone in Lyle's room, once reported being awakened in the middle of the night by a disturbing noise in her room. She opened her eyes to find that a wooden chair that had been placed against the wall, opposite the bed, was now leaning against her bed's mattress!

Another woman guest who had spent a night in Lyle's room stated that she had also been awakened one night to find a tall, slender man with a beard, and wearing a straw hat, standing next to the sink! When she spoke to him, he faded away.

Apparently, Lyle does not tolerate women's cosmetics in "his" room. He will routinely move them around the room to show his displeasure. We had a group of four couples, who were attending a golf tournament, stay as guests at the hotel. One of the women staying in Lyle's room approached me one morning and said, "Would you rather I not place my cosmetics on the dresser?" I was caught off guard by her question and answered, "No, not at all." I asked her to explain, and she told me that twice after leaving her make up on the dresser, she'd returned to the room to find it all in the sink! I assured her that I would check with the housekeeping staff. Upon questioning the staff, none of them mentioned moving the woman's cosmetics and dropping them in the sink.

Another time, we had a woman check into the room and

not more than 20 minutes later she returned to the front desk stating, "The strangest thing just took place in my room. As soon as I placed my box of makeup on the dresser, it 'hopped' onto the floor! It didn't fall, it hopped off!" This woman didn't know anything about Lyle, so I thought she'd enjoy hearing about him. I began to describe our resident ghost to her, and she was delightfully entertained by the story. Then another time a chef, who was employed at the hotel, was in the kitchen baking bread. He placed the dough in the oven and was apparently distracted by other work, because he totally forgot about checking the oven. He stated that without warning, and at the appropriate time, he was startled to see the oven door swing wide open, exposing the perfectly baked bread! It appeared as if Lyle was also volunteering his kitchen skills, making sure our chef was fully assisted. If you were to ask me, do I believe in the existence of ghosts, I would have to answer with a definite, yes! In the 12 years that we've been operating the hotel, we've only had two people who were bothered enough by Lyle to actually want to check out. That's a good record, I think. Believe it or not,

"She told me that twice after leaving her makeup on the dresser, she'd returned to the room and found all of it in the sink!"

Lyle's room is our most popular room. The public loves him. And, as I said before, we all love him. Although our resident cat, "Miss Fat Cat," does act strangely sometimes, as if some invisible person has been teasing her, our staff loves Lyle, and he's never touched, or done anything mean, to anyone.

SACRAMENTO

Framed by the Sacramento River to the west, Interstate 5 to the east, the Capitol Mall to the south, and the "I" Street Bridge to the north, Sacramento, California's capital city since 1854, is both rich with history and visually captivating. The Native Americans who inhabited the Sacramento area were from the Miwok, Maidu, and Shonommey nations. For thousands of years these people lived by hunting deer and gathering acorns, which constituted the bulk of their diets. The land was bountiful, and consuming only what they needed to survive, these resourceful men and women utilized all that was available to them. Acorns, a substantial part of their diet, were gathered, ground into flour, and leeched of their tannic acid through the repeated application of water. This mush was then cooked in

woven, water- tight baskets using heated stones that were placed into the moist, acorn mush. The stones were continuously stirred, and eventually the mush was cooked and made edible.

In the early 1800s, Gabriel Moraga, a Spanish explorer, gave the name "Sacramento," meaning Holy Sacrament, to the surrounding land and river. In the year 1848, the discovery of gold in Coloma changed the area and the native lifestyle forever. Sacramento became a center of urban activity. Large, mercantile buildings, as well as homes and pioneer supply warehouses, were established. The Sacramento River served the town well, and helped in the economic success of the town's development, as it was utilized as a route of commerce and transportation. As the railroad developed, the town became even more a center of commerce. But in the early 1850s, devastating fires and floods took their toll on the citizens. Even cholera made a deadly visit to the Sacramento Valley. Eventually, after four years, things began to get back to normal, and Sacramento grew in stature and Western prominence. Today, California's capitol reins supreme over an extraordinary state of magnificence.

SUTTER'S FORT

Sutter's Fort began as a small settlement, founded by John Sutter, a German-born Swiss entrepreneur, in 1839. This one-time, small, lowly gathering of settlers would come to mark a supremely important position in California's history and the great migration to the West.

John Sutter acquired the land grant for his settlement from the Mexican government and called it New Helvetia, meaning New Switzerland. However, the settlement generally became known, and was soon accepted as, Sutter's Fort. Self-sufficiency was paramount to the fort's survival.

The fort, primarily constructed by Native Americans who did the bulk of the labor, soon became widely known as a way station and trade center for pioneers. Another example of the fort's role in history was when it sent several rescue parties to help the doomed Donner Party that had been trapped in the Sierra Nevadas during the severe winter of 1846–47. Perhaps the most famous of its roles was in 1848, when John Sutter sent a work party to Coloma, to construct a lumber mill. During the building of the mill, construction foreman James Marshall spotted the glint of yellow gold among some stones. Efforts were made to keep the news of this discovery quiet, but to no avail. Soon word spread, and the rest of this worldwide rush of fortune seekers is now the basis of California's history.

Eight-year-old Donner Party survivor Patty Reed carried this doll across the plains to California. During the bitter months, snowbound in the Sierra Nevada mountains, Patty had "Dolly" to confide in and to comfort her. She later donated the doll to Sutter's Fort, the original destination of the Donner Party.

With much excitement and quick movement of Sutter's workers away from the fort in search of wealth, to the town of Coloma, the fort was soon left deserted. John Sutter was left without a work force, and by the 1880s, the fort's only original building—"The Central Building"—remained. The fort was reconstructed in 1891, based on an 1847 map. Sutter's Fort and the California State Indian Museum are both located in an easily-reached part of downtown Sacramento.

MICHAEL "SPARKY" ANDERSON'S STORY

I'm originally from the state of Michigan, and I've been at the fort now for about 12 years. I manage the fort's "Trade Store," also known as the gift shop. I'm also the Master Blacksmith, and I present public demonstrations of blacksmithing techniques from the gold-rush era.

It's commonly known among the staff that the fort was built upon a Miwok Native American gravesite. I remember, before working at the fort, I was told many stories about

The Central or Administration Building

the ghosts that dwell in the fort by several employees. Many of the ghost sightings center around the ghosts of a woman and a man, that are regularly seen at the Central Building. The Central Building, also known as the Administration Building, is the two-story adobe brick building, that incidentally, is the only original standing building within the fort complex. When spotted, these ghosts are seen standing in this building's doorways. I recall one Saturday night in 1989, when the employees, and docents, were involved in a two-day event at the fort. We all spent the night at the fort, and that was when I first heard about the ghosts of the man and woman who inhabit the Central Building.

At the entrance to each of the Central Buildings rooms, there is a pre-recorded explanation of what that particular room was historically used for. This tape-recorded explanation assists with the self-guided tour, and is programmed by a motion detector to automatically play as a person's body passes in front of each doorway.

At the Central Building, on the second floor, there is one room that has a window named the Doctor's Room. One of our docents told me that a woman's image reportedly has been seen by visitors, gazing out of this particular window. The ghost is reportedly only seen in the evening hours, dressed in early California-style gold-rush garb, from about the mid-1850s.

One especially interesting account from a witness who spotted our ghosts was told to me four years ago by a park visitor at the fort. The sighting took place in the summer of 1998, and involved a group of boy scouts. The group of scouts was visiting the fort from the San Francisco Bay Area. This group was accompanied by another group of scouts that was visiting from Guadalajara, Mexico. They came to the fort and set up quarters in the Central Building. After introducing myself, I engaged the Mexican Scout Master in conversation, at which time he began to tell me of a strange experience he had had at the fort.

"The ghosts can be seen standing in this building's doorways."

He reported to me that the previous afternoon he had been sitting alone on a bench on the upper floor of the Central

". . . a woman's image is reportedly seen."

Building. Strangely, the pre-recorded message had begun to play on its own, as if someone had passed in front of the motion detector. Again, the Scout Master stated that he had been the only person on the upper floor.

Suddenly, from the door opening on the west side of the room, two men had entered, dressed in period clothing. These men had walked past the seated Scout Master, and had quickly walked toward a wooden staircase. They had proceeded to walk up the staircase, where they had disappeared from his sight. The scout master said he immediately had thought these men were associated with a costumed fort reenactment of some kind, and had enjoyed the show.

His curiosity having been aroused, he had decided to follow these actors up the stairs, to the third floor. He had walked over to the stairs and had noticed that there was no way to walk up the stairs, because a barrier of framed wood and wire had obviously been constructed by the park service to prevent any unauthorized person from taking the stairs. Immediately he had felt unnerved, because how could the two men have walked

"The Scout Master said he immediately knew he had seen ghosts!"

so easily through this obvious barricade? The Scout Master said he had immediately known that he had seen ghosts, and that the experience had scared the devil out of him! He had quickly walked outside the building, to gather his senses, and soon he had located a park employee. Having described the incident, he had managed to convince the perplexed employee to follow him back inside the building, for the purpose of physically describing what he had just seen. The employee had been at a loss for words, and had had no reasonable explanation.

I have personally experienced the presence of a spirit the day I took over the fort's Blacksmith Shop. Between 1988–1989, there was a fellow who used to work at the Blacksmith Shop by the name of "Slow Wolf." Slow Wolf was directly involved in setting up the shop's iron furnace and display, and was also the main interpreter of the blacksmithing art. He also belonged to a "Mountain Man" organization, and the name "Slow Wolf" was the name he had given himself and chosen to identify with.

When Slow Wolf died, against the park rangers' directives a group of his friends scattered his cremated remains, or ashes, all about the fort's Blacksmith shop. I never met Slow Wolf, but

I have been told a lot about his unique history at the fort.

At the time, I was still very new to the blacksmithing trade. I recall working one day at the same Blacksmith Shop where Slow Wolf had worked, when something very peculiar took place. As I was busy at the table working on a project, I suddenly had the sensation of someone standing next to me, looking over my shoulder. I turned my head to see who it was, and spotted no one. Immediately, a prickly sensation came over me. I actually felt the physical presence of someone leaning over my shoulder to view my work! These creepy visits took place for a total of about six times during the first year that I worked in the shop.

"I personally experienced the 'presence' of a spirit"

I never did mention these experiences to any of my co-workers. I just decided to keep this information to myself. There was no pattern to these visits; day or night I'd suddenly feel the presence of what I believe were Slow Wolf's visits. I didn't hear any footsteps, or actually see a person standing next to me. I would just "feel" someone standing right beside me. I knew it must be Slow Wolf checking up on my blacksmithing work. I guess he was making sure I was operating the Blacksmith Shop in the same way he had done.

Before I began working at the fort, if someone had asked me if I believed in the existence of spirits, or ghosts, my answer would have been a definite no. But now I have to say, honestly, I'm not so sure. My curiosity makes me to want to experience seeing a ghost. Others have, so I guess I'd welcome the possibility too.

Shavehead, Chief of the Hat Creek, Atsugewi people. The Atsugewi's homeland was in the area now known as Lassen National Park.

CALIFORNIA STATE INDIAN MUSEUM

The museum is housed on the same two-block city location as Sutter's Fort. The museum houses one of the finest collections of California Native American basketry. From cooking or boiling, to flawlessly beautiful and delicately decorated, feather baskets, all regions of the state's Native American population are represented.

Other important items on display are musical instruments and ceremonial dance regalia. There are exhibits that also highlight tools, hunting and gathering implements, and contemporary art. The spirituality of California's native peoples is a dominant theme throughout the displays. Outside demonstrations include the Gathering of Honored Elders (held in May), the Art Show and Acorn Day (both held in Autumn), and the Arts and Crafts Holiday Fair (held Fridays and Saturdays after the Thanksgiving holiday).

LINDA BLUE'S STORY

I'm Miwok/Maidu from the Wilton Rancheria on the Consumnes River, located about 38 miles southeast of Sacramento. This year marks my third season that I've been working at the State Indian Museum. My official title is "On-call Park Aid" employee. I help out with the usual museum interpretation duties, such as describing to visitors the various rare California baskets, and other items of historical importance that are displayed. Before beginning my employment at the museum, I was told by fellow Native Americans about the history of adjacent Sutter's Fort being built upon a Native American burial mound. I know of several burial sites that have been disturbed around the fort area. Our museum is housed in a building just a short walk behind the fort. And working at the Indian Museum has not been a "spiritual" problem for me. Anthropologists have also discovered Native American artifacts

Linda Blue

on the grounds surrounding the museum and fort. I know from working on archaeological sites on my own reservation that our ancestral spirits do care about their belongings. Fortunately, the state is now sensitive to our beliefs, and Native American employees are given the option of being re-assigned to other sites if they wish. It's also well known that some Native Americans refuse to work at Sutter's Fort because of sudden, and unusual, illnesses that are reported by them, soon after entering the area. Because of this, today I can't name one Native American that I know who works at the fort. Employees have mentioned to me that they have seen dark figures walking in the museum, and on the museum grounds. Of course, I myself was hesitant at first to work so close to such a spiritual site. But, because I sincerely respect my ancestors, I know I'll be all right. What is disturbing is when non-natives dig up Native American burial sites, and disrespectfully take the offerings, such as the jewelry that the dead person was lovingly buried with. For instance, it was a common burial rite for Native American people to bury strings of handmade shell beads with their dead. We call these burial beads, "Cry Beads." I've seen these funeral beads being displayed, and sold, at swap meets and auctions. Some non-Native Americans can't seem to relate, as we do, to the spiritual significance that

"It was a common burial rite for Native American people to bury strings of hand-made shell beads with their dead. We call these burial beads, 'Cry Beads'."

these funeral items have to our culture. So they take our burial offerings, restring and sell them. It's very sad to see.

My own spiritual experiences at the museum are not un-common from those of others who have spent time any length of time there. For example, when I'm alone, standing at the front desk, soon after closing the doors for the day, I'll sometimes hear the soft sound of older, Native American women chanting a song. Their songs are most evident in the rear of the building, where old baskets are displayed behind glass. There will be times when I'll quietly walk to the rear of the museum, then pause for a few moments at the basket display. Soon I'll hear the spirit women singing in their native language. I don't recognize the language, but they're definitely Native American songs. The songs are not loud, but are more of a soothing, soft chanting. The chanting will continue without pause. As I walk back, returning to the front desk, I can still hear these women's voices. My explanation is that the chanting is due directly to the museum displays. Because the baskets being displayed have been collected from all over California, the singing spirit women could be from any one of the many Native American nations that existed in the state. Deep within my soul, I can "feel" these spirit women's connection, and attachment, to their baskets. I know they're checking to see that their work is being cared for, that it's being honored in the right way. It's almost as if they want their baskets to return home to their own people. Employees have also mentioned to me that they have seen dark figures, or shadows, walking among the museum displays, and also on the museum grounds. Other strange, but common, occurrences are the various artifacts that move on their own, within the museum. These particular Native American items on display are moved off shelves, as if the spirits are annoyed. Several times I've witnessed spoons, beads, and small baskets that I know have been securely attached to a pedestal, being moved off the pedestal, and onto the bottom of the case. Other things that have frightened employees, both Native and Anglo, have been the shaking of padlocks that hang on the cases. We've all seen this take place. We've stood by and watched as the locks that are mounted on the display cases move, as if some invisible hands were pulling, to forcibly open them. Our collective response has been, "We've got to get out of here. Something is not right!" As recently as three weeks ago, some employees came to me and reported that the padlocks on the cases were once again moving. So, as I said, it's a common experience. Not long ago, we had a group of about 100 gypsies visit the museum grounds. One gypsy woman came into the museum and engaged me in conversation about one of her family members who was in a local hospital. Immediately I felt a strange feeling come over me. I felt that something was not right. This woman had a strong spiritual presence about her, and it was affecting me in a negative manner. As she spoke, I felt her energy, or power, pushing against me. I actually felt her energy forcing me away from her. This was very strange, because it came over me without any warning. I moved several steps back, away from her, when something unseen, and very powerful, struck me from the side. Just then, another gypsy woman came to join her friend. Without them moving, or saying a word, I was moved from side to side by these women's power. Somehow, I escaped this spiritual "tug of war," and walked over to a fellow ranger who was standing nearby. I asked the ranger to take over because I wasn't feeling well. I knew these women were trying to tap into my spirit, and take my Native American power from me. Their power was very strong and hard to break away from. It was a terrible and strange moment for me. An experience that I've never had before. I'd hope the spirits who are attached to their baskets in our museum understand that we honor them, and their baskets. I think they do. Our people are very strong people. I enjoy being surrounded by my culture. We know how to identify and protect ourselves from bad spiritual things. We pray, and use sage to "smoke" our homes, and to honor our families. The "Chaw'se," or "Big Time" gathering at Indian Grinding Rock State Park in the Sierra Nevada Foothills is also a special, spiritual time for us. This gathering is attended by many Native American families from all areas of the state, and is primarily focused on unity and thanksgiving ceremonies.

OLD SACRAMENTO

Old Sacramento is a registered National Historic Landmark. Here you can find the state's greatest concentration of historic buildings. Adding to the historic charm are boardwalks made of thick, wide pine planks, instead of the more typical cement sidewalks. Built adjacent to the Sacramento River, on the west, this original city site provided convenient access to boats unloading their merchandise and to the eager citizens. The Gold Rush of 1849 transported the small town into a major area of new wealth and barter. Saloons were used as an exchange location for gold dust and nuggets into U. S. coins. As the gold rush boom began to wane, the Old Sacramento area became a gathering place for migrant workers, and the original pioneer businesses changed from bustling mercantile establishments to simple, unadorned warehouses. It fell into such a state of disrepair that during the mid-20th century, a wave of threateningly shoddy and trashy

bars and hotels succeeded to take hold. Sadly, the Old Sacramento area turned into one of the worst skidrows in the West. Fortunately, during the 1970s, a positive trend toward re-development gave Old Sacramento a dramatic, and much needed, new focus. A major reconstruction project was begun, and at the end, Old Sacramento took its place as a living link to California's historic past.

Today, Old Sacramento offers its visitors many diversions and museums. Four prominent museums of note are: The Discovery Museum History Center, The California State Railroad Museum, The Wells Fargo History Museum, and the California Military Museum.

PATRICIA BAEZ'S STORY

In September of 1993, my husband, Lorenzo, and I decided to take a three-week trip from our home in San Diego and travel up the California coast. At the time, I was also in need of a change of employment from my job as a surgery nurse at Scrips Medical Center in San Diego. Deciding to mix business with a pleasurable vacation, I took a folder full of resumés, which I dropped off at hospitals along the way. We had been thinking of relocating to a new city for months, and decided that the farthest north in California we would consider resettling would be Sacramento. After two weeks of traveling up the state, we eventually arrived in Sacramento and checked into a hotel. After breakfast, we toured the city and the State Capitol building, had lunch, then did a little more touring. The next day we met with a realtor, and eventually found a house on the south side of town, which we bought, and have lived in ever since. To celebrate our house purchase, after we had signed the house contract that evening, we decided to visit Old Sacramento, where

we enjoyed a wonderful dinner at a nice restaurant. The time was around 8 p.m. As we left the restaurant, Lorenzo suggested we take a stroll around the Old Town area. As we walked on the western boardwalk, we spotted the rail yard, and the display of an actual steam locomotive. I remember how the old fashion light poles were lit, the romantic glow they gave off, and shadows they cast about the yard. It was a perfect evening.

As we walked arm in arm toward the locomotive, I mentioned to Lorenzo that aside from another couple seated some distance from us, we were the only others in the area. I asked Lorenzo if we could sit down on the bench, under the large, metal shelter that protectively hung over the locomotive. We sat and talked for a few minutes, and noticed when the other couple got up and walked away. Lorenzo got up and walked to the locomotive while I remained on the bench smoking a cigarette. He busied himself investigating the wheels and smoke stack of the immense machine. I was gazing at the beautiful buildings across the street, and allowing my imagination to place me in the era of the 1800s, when the town must have been quite a busy, and colorful, place. The architecture of the buildings, the boardwalk, and the darkness of the night easily allowed me to grasp the feeling of that era, and what it might have looked like. Lorenzo came over to me and said he was going to look for a public bathroom, or else return to the restaurant where we had had dinner, and use their men's room. I didn't feel like getting up, so I told him that I would just wait for him as I sat on the bench. I watched as he walked away. Recalling all the traveling that we had recently done, I felt a very peaceful feeling of contentment, and accomplishment, come over me. As I was thinking all these thoughts, I noticed a small man in a dark suit walking on the boardwalk quite a distance from me. I saw him pause twice to open his coat and check for something in his pocket. Because he was the only person in the area, and I was by myself, my eyes were focused, and did not leave him. I also noticed that he had a strange manner of walking. He walked with a bounce to each step, and as I said, I kept my eyes on him because, after all, he was a little strange looking. He walked a few steps up to the window of a closed shop and, when he turned around to face my direction, I spotted a bag he was holding. From where I was sitting, I thought it was a bag, but it could have been something else. At any rate, I wasn't able to make out clearly what the heck it was. He made his way back to the street, and then on toward the railroad station that was just a few yards away from where I was seated.

I was not afraid, or even concerned for my safety. I could see that the man was not very tall. In fact, I was much taller than he, so I didn't believe he posed any real threat to me. But, my demeanor suddenly changed when the strangest thing became clear to me. As this stranger came closer, I noticed his footsteps were not making any sound! The street is composed of dirt with a top layer of gravel, so walking on this would naturally make a sound of some sort. But there was absolutely no sound to his steps!

As fear started to well up inside me, I didn't dare take my eyes off the dark stranger. I suddenly began to feel very vulnerable sitting there alone on that bench. My instincts told me this little man was not normal, and might even be a ghost. Slowly he came, approaching my direction. I attempted to stay very quiet, and to make myself as invisible as possible. I threw my lit cigarette to the ground, and with my right foot, slowly extinguished it. As he came closer, he appeared very frail, and slightly bent over, because he produced a little shaking motion with each step. Again, I noticed that his footsteps did not made any sound. I was ready for anything to happen. Ready to immediately jump off the bench and run for my life! Fortunately, he turned about 50 feet away from me, and headed straight for the door of the railroad station building. He stood at the door, and as I watched, he extended

"He made his way toward the railroad station that was just a few yards away from where I was seated."

his hand to reach for the doorknob. I heard him fumbling and pulling the knob, then he walked inside. When I say he walked inside, I mean he walked inside without opening the door. He just passed through the closed door! I froze. Coincidentally, Lorenzo appeared at that moment, exactly at the same spot on the boardwalk where I had first spotted the ghost. I yelled at him from where I sat, demanding he hurry and come over to me. When he got to my side, I hugged him and began to tell him what I had just witnessed. He of course did not believe me, and even jokingly made fun of my story. But, because of how distressed I must have appeared, he soon stopped with the jokes. With his arm around me, we quickly began to walk away from the rail yard, as l repeated over and over the words, "I know what I saw, that was a ghost Lorenzo, that was a ghost!" Just then, my storytelling abruptly ended when we both heard the sound of invisible scraping and scuffling footsteps, coming from the area where I had seen the ghost of the little man disappear. There was no one anywhere to be seen. Lorenzo also heard the ghostly sounds, and he quickly took hold of my hand, then ordered me to run. We practically flew across the street to our car. I don't know of anyone else who has had a similar experience at the rail-yard like I had had. I've lived in Sacramento for several years now, and no one has mentioned any such ghost stories to me. Maybe people are afraid to come forward with what they've experienced. I do know that I won't ever go out there at night again. It all seems so strange and unnerving to me now, having to recall my experience, even though it happened over eight years ago.

Placerville

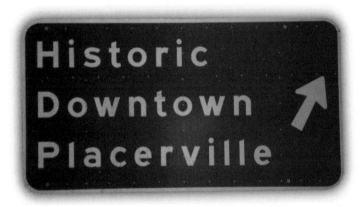

Originally, the town was known by the name, "Old Dry Diggings." This name soon was changed to the more macabre "Hangtown," due to its citizens' infamous over-zealous practice of justice. The citizens of Hangtown eventually changed the town's name to Placerville. The town is bordered to the north and south by the rivers Middle Fork, Rubicon, Consumnes, and South Fork. Because of this opportune location Placerville enjoyed prosperous growth and notoriety. The discovery of gold in the nearby town of Coloma, and the subsequent gold rush, swelled Placerville's population almost overnight. Placerville has remained the county seat of El Dorado County since 1854, and is the gateway to South Lake Tahoe. Ongoing industries in the area range from gold mining, farming of fruit and Christmas trees, wineries, and lime. Today, many gift shops, restaurants, and bakeries entice locals and visitors alike to this diverse and historic community.

Ruby W. DeCair's Story

My husband and I have been the owners of the Hangman's Tree Bar for more than 20 years. Originally we lived in San Francisco, but in 1967 we moved to Placerville. Before we purchased it, we were never told about anything paranormal taking place in the bar, except for a local psychic who did speak about getting a "vibration" from a male ghost who had taken up residence. Apparently, this ghost was one of several law breakers who had been executed on the hanging tree, which once grew in this location. That historic hanging tree did in fact grow on the property, directly where the bar was built. Right over there, where the bar's jukebox now sits, directly underneath the floor, remains the old stump of that actual tree. In the late 1840s most of the town, including the tree, was destroyed by a great fire. Because of the extensive fire damage, the tree was cut down to its stump.

"Right over there, where the jukebox now sits, directly underneath the floor, you'll find the old stump of that actual tree."

My own personal ghost experience happened early one morning, as I was opening the bar. The time was 5:30 as I walked inside through the front door. Immediately, I spotted a strange looking man sitting at a table, in a chair. He surprised me. He caught me off guard because I obviously didn't expect to see anyone in my bar, especially when it had been locked up. And when I spotted him, he didn't speak a single word to me, which was odd. I noticed he was wearing a black suit with a black top hat. He appeared to be solid, just like any living person might appear. Initially, he didn't give me the impression that I was staring at a ghost, but once he turned his head, and our eyes met, my impression changed. I knew something was not right. Fear did begin to take over me. Without delaying another minute, I hurriedly turned around, and quickly made my way back outside. Soon my rationality took over, and I got the courage to again reopen the door. I entered, and carefully looked around, investigating all the areas of the bar. Then I walked to the rear of the bar, checking to make sure the back-door lock

Historic Hangman's Tree Bar

had not been broken. I didn't find a trace of the stranger.

Now, as I think back on that day, I find it interesting to know that I actually saw a real ghost. My husband, Jim, doesn't believe in ghosts. He's told me that if word got out about our ghost, it would drive customers away. I personally don't think that's true, because the public enjoys knowing such things. I think people are intrigued by ghosts. My employees have also had numerous experiences with the ghost, especially our night bartender, who doesn't work here any longer. You know, we're not the only ones in town with ghosts. The Diamond Hotel has some, as does our City Chamber of Commerce building. I know that there are ghosts that walk up and down Main Street. They're here, but these sightings are now just so common, that we don't talk much about them any longer. You know, people who don't believe think we're just dreaming them up. But they're here all right. They're here.

TUOLUMNE

In 1848 the Reverend James Wood discovered gold in Tuolumne County, near present-day Jamestown. Just one year later, thousands of miners invaded the numerous county's streams and gulches, setting up camps and seeking their fortunes in the hard rock mine business. Soon, permanent stone, brick, and wood buildings began to replace the miners' canvas tents. The established new town of Sonora sprang from this wealth of venture seekers, and in no time the town became the county seat, as it remains to this day. As World War I broke out, newcomers settled in the area, and tried their luck at the more stable logging and ranching business. Tuolumne soon became the center of California's timber industry. In 1897 the railroad came into Tuolumne County and began another definite boom, which benefitted both the mining and timber industries. In its more recent history, the Hollywood film industry discovered Tuolumne County, and used its scenic beauty for various movie and television productions. Since the 1960s, many visitors have discovered that the area is a beautiful, and somewhat affordable, place to retire.

ROBERT AND NANCE BELL'S STORY

When the actual day arrived for my wife, Nance, and me to make the move out of Fresno, we thought long and hard about retiring to the town of Kingman, Arizona, where our daughter and her family had moved a few years before. However, the more we thought about this possibility, the more it just didn't make much sense for us to pick up, and move, several hundred miles away to an unfamiliar town. Having both lived and worked all our lives up to that point in California, it was difficult to imagine moving out of the state and starting over in Arizona. Being in our mid 60s, our options were limited, to a great extent. So when we did sell our home, we looked for a nice, quiet, rural community not far from Fresno, in the gold rush area of Northern California. Well, the day arrived, and the three of us—Nance, myself, and our small dog, Cindy—got into our RV and traveled into the Sierra Nevada mountain range of the state. We located a realtor, and searched for about two weeks, investigating all the small towns in the area. Our real estate agent in the town of Sonora eventually located a quaint, little three-bedroom house, with four acres, in the southeastern area of Calaveras county, not far from the small town of Tuolumne. Nance and I knew immediately this was where we would make our new home. Because of its age, the house was in need of a few upgrades, but nothing that would mean any major work. On the property was a detached garage, a workshop, and a chicken house made of wood and rusted wire and hinges. Over the years, from lack of use and neglect, half the chicken house had fallen to the ground. I was drawn to it from the start. I guess its strangely familiar design brought back old memories of my childhood in Nebraska. My family raised a breed of chicken, named Barred Rock. My grandmother was very fond of a particular coop that grandfather had made, similar to the one on this property. The uniqueness of the wire-enclosed run, the nesting boxes being stacked on four levels, and

"The chicken coop was almost an exact replica."

where the door was located on the east side, rekindled wonderful childhood memories for me.

While Nance got busy with the task of decorating the house, and replanting the garden with new bulbs, and doing general landscaping, I got busy with personalizing the other three buildings, which included the chicken house. We wanted to keep a few chickens for the benefit of having fresh organic eggs, so I knew I would soon have to fix up that old chicken house. When we moved onto the property, I didn't notice anything strange, or out of the ordinary, that I could label ghostly or paranormal. But on the other hand, Nance did have such an experience. She once mentioned hearing someone's footsteps walking in the middle of the night throughout the house. She didn't place much importance on this, until the frightening experience we both had one early evening, while sitting in our living room. At that time we had been living in the house for about three weeks. The time was about 6 or 7 p.m., and I was writing a letter to my sister. Nance was reading a new gardening book she had borrowed from a neighbor. Quite suddenly, we heard something moving about in the kitchen. I stopped writing and paused to listen closely. Nance glanced up from her book and softly said, "Robert, did you hear that?" I answered, "Stay still, it's probably a mouse, I'll go see where it is." As soon as I had got up off my chair, we both heard a male voice begin to speak unintelligible words in a whispered tone. It was coming from the kitchen. "Don't panic," I said. "Just stay where you are." I walked to the kitchen, and because there was still enough sunlight coming into the room to make things visible, I didn't bother to switch on the light. But when I entered the kitchen, I immediately noticed the strange, overpowering odor of stale sweat. As I searched around our small kitchen, looking for any animal or human evidence, I checked the door leading out to the backyard. It was locked. I looked up and glanced out through the small window built into the door, but I didn't notice anything unusual in the yard. Suddenly, I heard the sound of a cabinet door open to my right, and as I turned around toward the sink, I spotted Nance standing by the entrance to the kitchen. Nance was pointing at the kitchen cabinet, wanting me to take notice of something. The cabinet door began to slowly open on its own, and then it opened with a quick swing. This was followed by the door next to it, which also quickly opened. Without thinking I ran to Nance's side. The quiet in the room was intense. Something was definitely not right. Call it a ghost, or spirit, but I became a believer at that very instant. At that time I didn't believe in the paranormal. Or I should say, it wasn't so much that I didn't disbelieve in such things as ghosts or spirits, but was more that I had never seen any. Like most people, I needed proof.

I knew Nance felt the same way as I did about ghosts. From time to time, we've both had friends come to us with crazy stories about things they've read, or what they heard on television, but overall we just were not the type of people who believed in such things. But what my wife and I both experienced that day

"It moved off the sill and came crashing to the floor, sending glass shards everywhere!"

caused us to rethink the whole "ghost thing."

I quickly moved over to the cabinet, and thinking I might spot a small animal, I carefully looked inside and saw nothing. I closed the doors and turned to Nance. "What the hell was that?" I said. Nance answered, "Robert we have a ghost. What are we going to do?" Immediately, a small, glass vase with flowers that Nance had set on the window sill moved off the sill and came crashing to the floor, sending glass shards everywhere! Instinctively I yelled, "Okay, you can leave us alone now. Do you hear, we want you to leave us alone." As soon as I had finished those words, we heard the same man's ghostly voice speak, whispering "Damn you Robert, damn you Robert." Just as before, the atmosphere in the kitchen was thick with the odor of stale sweat. Nance looked at me, then walked out towards the living room and sat motionless in her chair. I asked, "What just happened in there? Nance, you heard the voice too, didn't you?" Nance responded, "Yes, and I think we have a big problem, Robert. I don't think it was smart of you to anger the spirit like you did." I attempted to convince Nance that I was not wanting to argue with any ghost, but seeing that Nance was under a lot of stress, I let it go. After that first encounter with the spirit, I had another unusual occurrence. One morning, four days later, after breakfast, I took a short walk to where the chicken house was. I loaded up the wheelbarrow with screws, nails, hammer, wire, and a saw. Whoever built the chicken house must have been a very precise woodworker, because on closer inspection, I noticed the expertly made clean-cut notches and framing the builder had made. This was not just a regular chicken house; it was crafted to be a very nice piece work, one to be proud of. Having worked on a few wood projects myself, I could appreciate that.

Over the years, and through many seasons of snow and summer sun, the structure had weathered well through these changes. A few rotted boards and hinges were in need of replacement, as was the roof, but except for this and some new galvanized wire, not much more would be needed—just the chickens. I got busy with the necessary repair work and because of my intense concentration, I didn't even notice the hours pass by. At about

"A few rotting boards and hinges were in need of replacement."

1:30 p.m. as I glanced at my watch, I expected Nance soon would be calling me to the house for lunch. I decided to leave what I was doing to get some food in me, and walked back to the house. As I placed my saw on top of an old wood box, I noticed a piece of red cloth a few feet away, protruding out from underneath a fallen nest box. It caught my interest, and I decided to pull it out of the dirt. At first, I thought it was an old shirt.

I held one corner of the box, and as I reached down, suddenly I spotted a rattlesnake! I must have jumped about three feet off the ground! It gave me quite a fright. I quickly dropped the box, but soon regained my senses, and watched as the snake harmlessly slithered away, disappearing into the brush. I made

"I picked it up and began to unwrap the faded, rotted cloth."

"A small leather wallet!"

quite sure the snake had moved on. I used a long stick to tap the nest box, then reached in for the red cloth.

As I pulled on one corner of the cloth, I noticed it was a handkerchief. I soon discovered the handkerchief had been used to wrap some small, square object. As I gave a stronger tug on the handkerchief, it tore away from my hand (over time the cloth had rotted and was covered in mildew). Using my stick, I moved the wrapped object away from the box, then pushed it out onto the ground. I picked it up, and began to unwrap the faded, rotted cloth.

It didn't take much effort to remove the cloth and soil from what I could now see was a small leather wallet. I carefully opened the wallet, and could tell by its condition that it was very old. It was made up of just one compartment, or pocket—not like a wallet of the modern-day type, with its slots for credit cards, and a plastic view window for a driver's license. This was, for its time, a practical man's wallet for carrying bills and not much else.

I carried the wallet out into the bright sunlight, away from the shaded canopy of black oak trees where the chicken house was located, and leaned my back against a tree. There, I opened the wallet and found three things that the mold had not completely rotted away. There was a short, personal letter with the words written in pencil, "Tom, you need to meet the cart from Sacramento on the 14th. Iron straps. The office will pay your fee at the gate. Don't be late." This letter was dated August 6, 1943, and was signed, "Howard." The second thing I found tucked in the wallet's pocket was a U. S. $1. 00 bill. The last item that was tucked into one corner pocket was a small metal crucifix. That was all. I discovered nothing to identify the owner's name or address. Upon entering the house a few minutes later, I showed Nance what I had found. She looked at the wallet and said, "I bet someone stole it, then forgot where they had placed it, other-

"I leaned my back against a tree."

wise why would it be inside of a chicken's nest box?" Nance held the wallet in her hand, then lifted it to her nose, "Robert, have you taken a good sniff at this. Doesn't it remind you of something?" She said. Her words jarred my memory. I took it from her and sure enough the wallet's musty odor scent was exactly the same odor that we had both smelled when we had had our ghostly visit in the kitchen just a few days before. I have to say that I was a bit unnerved at that point.

I decided then and there, that the best place to take the wallet would be out, and away, from the house. Without wasting any time, I got up from the table and walked straight outside to the garage. I placed the wallet inside a small cardboard box, and placed the box on a shelf, where it has stayed to this day. One evening, about a week or so later, at about 8 p.m., we were both in the front yard. Nance was watering her new flower beds, and I was sitting on the stairs. We were talking about what we would focus on next in terms of improving the property. I suggested we remove a large tree that over the years was now more than 50-percent rotted away. Instead of describing to Nance how I would go about sawing away certain branches, I asked her to follow me out to the backyard so I could specifically show her. Nance turned off the water, and as we began to walk to the backyard, our dog, Cindy, ran up ahead of us and began to bark uncontrollably. As we neared the tree, Cindy came running back to us, and ceased her barking. Immediately we thought a cat or squirrel had frightened her. As I reached down to comfort our dog, I noticed she nervously jumped away from my hand and focused her attention on the area where the clump of trees, and chicken house, were. Both Nance and I also turned our attention to where our dog was focused, and what we saw scared the hell out of us!Standing there by the chicken house was the ghostly image of a man walking very slowly around the shrubbery. The image had a phosphorescent glow to it. Not a very bright light, just enough for us to make out its form, and to know this was a man. At one point he bent down, then straightened up, continuing his walk. He didn't wear a hat, or any other identifying clothing. It was just the outline of a man's figure. Nance and I spoke in whispered voices. I said, "Can this be true? Nance, we're actually seeing a ghost!" Nance said, "I knew something was not right. And I bet this might have something to do with the wallet." Somehow I gained the strength to yell out to the ghost, "Hey, hey there, what are you doing? What are you doing over there?" The ghost gave no indication that it heard me, it just continued to walk about the area in an aimless manner. We continued to watch it, mesmerized by it, for about two minutes. I had no need to walk on over and confront it. Our dog, Cindy, with an occasional whimper now and then, laid on the grass next to Nance and watched the ghost with us. I told Nance I was going to phone a neighbor and have them come on over to watched the ghost with us. Obviously, the ghost was not going away, so we

"What would a ghost want with a wallet that only has $1.00 in it?"

might as well have more witnesses. As I walked into the house, I switched on a light and reached for the phone. I heard Nance yell out, "Robert, it just disappeared!" Just at that moment, the strong odor of sweat came into the room. I decided not to "tempt" the ghost any further. I spoke out loud, "Okay, no problem, we're not going to bother you, just please go back outside!" Nance came into the house and without me saying anything, she said, "Robert, the smell is back, can you smell it?" I said, "Yes, I can. Hurry and turn on all the lights in the house." The odor lingered in the house for about 10 minutes, all the time giving us the unsettling feeling that the ghost was in the house with us. Happily, nothing was moved or broken. Eventually the odor left, and we had no further activity. As of today, the odor and apparition have not come back. We've lived on the property for close to six years now. Nance and I have discussed the possibility that maybe the wallet has something to do with the ghost. But what would a ghost want with a wallet that only had a note and a $1.00 bill? We have spoken to our daughter and a neighbor about the ghost, but they just listened to our story and had nothing meaningful to say.

We've discovered that it's not too difficult for us to live with a ghost. I have 14 laying hens in the chicken house now, and like I said, since the last incident, my wife and I have not had any more visits from the ghost. I just make sure to feed and care for the chickens during the daylight hours. No way am I going to venture out there when the sun goes down. I don't want anymore encounters with spirits, or rattlesnakes. No way! Maybe now that we've told our story, things might start up again. I sure hope not. I'm not sure how I would react the third time I experience something like that. I just think to myself there is another life besides this one. Beyond that, there is not much more I can say.

Yosemite
National Park

Yosemite Valley

Often called "the incomparable Valley," Yosemite Valley may be
the world's best-known example of a glacier-carved canyon.
The dramatic scale of its leaping waterfalls, rounded domes,
massive monoliths, and towering cliffs, has inspired painters,
poets, photographers, and millions of visitors. The park em-
braces a great tract of scenic wildlands set aside in 1890 to preserve a portion of the Sierra Nevada that stretches along
California's eastern flank. Ranging from 2,000 feet above sea
level to more than 13,000 feet, the park encompasses alpine
wilderness, groves of giant sequoia trees, and the Yosemite
Valley. The valley's sheer walls and flat floor evolved as alpine
glaciers lumbered through the canyon of the Merced River. The
ice carved through weaker sections of granite, plucking and
scouring rock but leaving intact harder portions, such as El

Capitan and Cathedral Rocks. Glaciers greatly enlarged the canyon that the Merced River had carved through successive uplifts of the Sierra. When the last glacier melted, its terminal moraine, left at its farthest advance into the valley, dammed up the melting water to form ancient Lake Yosemite in the newly carved U-shaped valley. Eventually sediment filled in the lake, forming today's flat valley floor.

Today, Yosemite Valley is a mosaic of open meadows sprinkled with wildflowers and flowering shrubs, oak woodlands, and mixed-conifer forests of ponderosa pine, incense cedar, and Douglas Fir. Wildlife—from monarch butterflies to mule deer and black bears—flourishes in these diverse communities. Waterfalls around the valley's perimeter reach their maximum flow in May and June. Most prominent are the Yosemite, Bridalveil, Vernal, Nevada, and Ililouette falls, but some have little or no water from mid-August through early fall. Meadows, riverbanks, and oak woodlands are sensitive and have been severely damaged by long-term human use.

Native American people have lived in the Yosemite region for as long as 8,000 years. By the mid-19th century, when native residents had their first contact with non-Native American people,

A lifelike statue of Chris Brown, "Chief Lemee" Southern Miwok 1900–1956, welcomes visitors to the museum

Chris Brown (Chief Lemee) dancing for park visitors in the Indian Village behind the Yosemite Museum, June 20, 1949.

they were primarily of Southern Miwok ancestry. However, trade with the Mono Paiutes from the east side of the Sierra for *pinon* pine nuts, obsidian, and other materials from the Mono Basin resulted in many unions between the two nations.

Chris Brown (1900–1956) was a Miwok born in Yosemite Valley. Known as "Chief Lemme," he performed Miwok dances for visitors to Yosemite from the 1920s until 1953. The dance regalia he is shown wearing is a mixture of Southern and Northern Miwok style. He also made and used a Paiute, or Plains-style drum, which he decorated with designs of his own creation.

Demonstrations of Native American culture have long been popular with visitors to Yosemite. The Indian Village, located behind the museum, was built in the late

Actual photograph of Chief Lemee wearing a shoulder cape of great horned owl feathers, clamshell disc beads, and a bone whistle around his neck.

1920s and is open year-round. Although daily demonstrations of Miwok dances are no longer presented, demonstrations of Miwok and Paiute culture take place there during the summer.

The native people of Yosemite developed a complex culture rich in tradition, religion, songs, and political affiliations. Making use of the varied local ecosystems, they used plant and animal resources to the best of their abilities. The pattern of oaks and grassland noted by early visitors to Yosemite Valley is probably a direct result of the intentional burning of underbrush practiced by native people.

MARIPOSA BATTALION ENTERS YOSEMITE VALLEY

Although the first sighting of Yosemite Valley by non-Native American people was probably by members of the Joseph Walker Party in 1833, the first actual known entry into the valley was not until nearly 20 years later. After the discovery of gold in the Sierra Nevada foothills in 1849, thousands of miners came to the Sierra to seek their fortune. Their arrival resulted in deadly, racial conflicts with local native people who bravely fought to protect their homelands. Because of such interaction, the Mariposa Battalion was organized as an expedition under the authority of the State of California to inflict punishment on Native Americans, and ultimately bring an end to the "Mariposa Indian War." The Battalion marched into the Yosemite Valley searching for Native Americans on March 27, 1851.

EARLY TOURISTS AND SETTLERS

Writers, artists, and photographers spread the fame of "the Incomparable Valley" throughout the world. A steadily increasing stream of strangers came on foot and horseback, and later by stagecoach. Realizing he could make money off of these people, James Hutchings became one of Yosemite's first entrepreneurs. Hotels and residences were constructed, livestock grazed in meadows where for centuries only deer browsed, orchards were planted, and as a result, Yosemite Valley's ecosystem suffered drastically. Native Americans could only watch with heavy-hearted disappointment as their sacred falls, meadows, trees, animals, and mountains were overrun with these invaders.

PROTECTION IS SOUGHT FOR YOSEMITE

Inspired by the scenic beauty of Yosemite, and spurred on by the specter of private exploitation of Yosemite's natural wonders, conservationists appealed to Senator John Conness of California. On June 30, 1864, President Abraham Lincoln signed a bill granting Yosemite Valley, and the Mariposa Grove of Giant Sequoias, to the State of California as an inalienable public trust. This was the first time in history that a federal government had set aside scenic lands simply to protect them, and for the purpose of people's enjoyment. This idea was the spark that helped Yellowstone become the first official national park a few years later, in 1872. Later, John Muir's struggle against the devastation of the sub-alpine meadows surrounding Yosemite Valley, resulted in the creation of Yosemite National Park on October 1, 1890. Military units with headquarters in Wawona, administered the park while the State of California continued to govern the area covered by the original 1864 grant. Dual control of Yosemite came to an end in 1906, when the State of California receded Yosemite Valley and the Mariposa Grove to the

federal government. Civilian park rangers took over from the military in 1914. Two years later, on August 25, 1916, through the persistent efforts of Steven Mather and Horace Albright, Congress authorized the creation of the National Park Service. This department office was to administer all national parks "in such manner and by such means, as to leave them unimpaired for the enjoyment of future generations."

Around the turn of the century, Hetch Hetchy Valley became the center of a bitter political struggle when the City of San Francisco wanted to dam the Tuolumne River inside Yosemite National Park, as a source of drinking water and hydroelectric power. In 1913, conservationists led by John Muir lost the battle when Congress passed the Raker Act, authorizing the construction of O'Shaughnessy Dam.

INCREASING VISITATION REQUIRES
MANAGEMENT PLANS
The day of the horse-drawn stagecoach drew to a close in 1907 with the construction of the Yosemite Valley Railroad from Merced to El Portal. While a few automobiles entered the park in 1900 and 1901, they were not officially permitted until 1913. In order to reduce competitive expansion of facilities in the park,

in 1925 two major concessionaires were consolidated into the Yosemite Park and Curry Company. As more and more people visited Yosemite Valley, the park began to suffer. People camped at random throughout its beautiful meadows, and the ever-increasing automobile traffic that haphazardly entered such fragile areas left the Valley eroded and drastically changed. As visitation, and the need for year-round services, increased, Yosemite Village was relocated from a place in the flood plain on the south side of the Merced River to the present Yosemite Village site to the north. Visitation for the first time  exceeded one million in 1954, and by 1976 more than two million people had visited Yosemite. In mid 1990, visitation topped four million. In the early 1970s, the National Park Service established one-way road traffic patterns, eliminated cars in the far east end of the Valley, offered free shuttle bus transportation in the Valley, converted the parking lot in front of the Valley Visitor Center to a pedestrian mall, and generally encouraged visitors to enjoy the park by walking or using public transportation.

Yosemite's General Management Plan, which was completed in 1980, articulated the needs for park-wide visitor services, resources management, interpretation services, concessions management, and park operations.

SAVINA CORBALLI'S STORY

I've worked and lived at the park since 1994. What began as a housekeeping or maid position, has since turned out to be my career. My girlfriend and I both began working at the park

together after we completed two years of college. We were looking for summer jobs, and were told by a friend that Yosemite
was always hiring summer, seasonal workers. We applied and
were soon hired at Curry Village as maids. Although my girlfriend returned to finish college, I decided to stay on at the park.
It's now been over seven years since that summer. Though I
haven't made much money throughout the years, I have managed to save a few dollars. My meals and rent for a one-bed-
room cabin are both deducted from my salary, and I know I'll
never get rich working here, but working in such a beautiful en-
vironment like Yosemite more than makes up for my lack of
salary. I've had several weird experiences at the park. A lot of
these experiences have not given me much cause to fear ghosts,
but one in particular sure made me change my mind. This "special" experience began in the spring of 1997, while I was hiking by myself in the back country of Tuolumne Meadows. I've
hiked many of the back trails, before, and I especially enjoy the
John Muir Trail. This has undoubtedly got to be among the
most beautiful hiking trails in the world!

The meadows are beautiful in the springtime, and the
spring of '97 was no different. I decided to hike alone, with only
my backpack and adventurous spirit. It's not at all unusual for
the employees at the park to do a solitary hike. Eventually, most
of the employees get the urge to explore the park, and because
of the availability of good trails, and time off from work, we
definitely take advantage of our beautiful location. However,
mutual friends' employment schedules don't always match, so
hiking alone is not uncommon.

One spring evening, I got all my gear ready for the six-day
hike that I had planned. On day two of my hike, I reached my
destination and set up my base camp. This is where I would be
spending three wonderful days alone, swimming in the streams,
hiking, and sleeping. What a life! I also brought two books with
me, one that was written about the history of Yosemite Park,

and one that was written about the Native Americans of the gold rush country. This second book basically wrote about the sad history and ultimate extermination of the Native Americans. I wanted to get a perspective of what most Americans don't learn in school. I know I certainly didn't get much of an education throughout my school years regarding the treatment of the native peoples of California. Like most visitors to Yosemite, I fell in love with the beauty of the area, and was unaware of its terrible history regarding the white man's treatment toward the Native Americans. I decided to take the opportunity on my hike to read and educate myself in this area. I also brought along a camera to take lots of pictures.

Coinciding with my hike, the park service was sponsoring a photography contest for non-professionals and I decided to enter. The first prize of $500 was something I wanted to take a chance on winning. So I brought alone about eight rolls of film. Everything went well on my hike, but on the the second day, things definitely took a different turn.

It was a warm afternoon, and I was lying on my sleeping bag inside my tent. As I was reading my book, I began to hear the footsteps of someone walking up to my camp. I glanced out of the tent and saw no one. This bothered me to the point that I got up, and walked outside of my tent to take a look around. I saw nothing. I thought perhaps it might be a squirrel, a raccoon, or a bird. But the footsteps were the sound a human walking would make, of someone placing one foot in front of the other. Even though the day was clear and bright, I saw no one around my camp.

I disregarded this minor incident and decided to take a short walk to the nearby stream. As I splashed myself with the cool, stream water, I began to think about my earlier experience with the footsteps. Subconsciously, the incident was still bothering me. I decided to walk back to my tent and get a snack.

As I rose and turned in the direction of my camp, which was about a quarter of a mile away, I noticed that someone was standing by the tent. I could tell it was a young guy wearing blue shorts and a blue cap, who was holding an orange backpack. I yelled out, "Can I help you?" The guy turned his head to look in my direction. I held up my arm and made a waving gesture to communicate that I had my eyes on him. He said nothing, and made no movement, other than to face in my direction, to indicate he knew I was yelling at him. I felt a bit alarmed, unsure of what he might be up to, or what I should do next, so I yelled once more, "That's my tent, can I help you?" Keep in mind, I was alone in the woods, so I didn't want to necessarily get too close to this strange guy. I'm smart enough to know that there are lots of weirdos who would like to take advantage of a single woman in a situation like this.

When he failed to respond to my calls, I knew, and felt something was definitely not right. I decided that the best thing for me to do was to stay put. Then he slowly turned away, and walked toward the open foot trail directly above my camp. I kept my eyes on this weird guy, while at the same time, wasted no time, briskly making my way to my tent.

Arriving, I looked over everything inside and outside the tent. It soon became clear to me that everything was untouched. Though strangely, there was an area of water soaking the ground, directly below where this guy had been standing.

Hoping to get a better glimpsed of him, I looked in the direction of the footpath. I spotted him, then noticed something unusual in the way he was walking. He moved abruptly from side to side, kind of staggering with each step. I imagined this guy might be drunk, or under the influence of drugs.

I sat down on the ground and observed as he made his way a few more feet, until he slowly disappeared. And when I say disappeared, I mean DISAPPEARED! The path was located in an open meadow without any trees, or large rocks to hide behind. It was midday without any shadows. The sun was bright and high in the sky. This guy was there one second, and then gone the next. He just disappeared!

I quickly stood up, thinking he must have taken a fall, and cautiously walked over to where he might have hit the ground. There was no evidence of the guy anywhere. No cap, no backpack, nothing! The meadow grasses and flowers were only about a foot or so high, so he couldn't have been hiding among the plants. I didn't want to contemplate the situation any longer. I knew that the only explanation was that I had been visited by a ghost. And it had appeared to me in broad daylight no less! Admittedly, this shook me up. And as I returned to my tent, I decided to cut my stay short, pack up my things, and return back home.

As I gathered up my belongings, I noticed drops of blood on the paper bags I had next to my camp stove and by the side of my tent. These were fresh drops, and there was only one way they could have gotten there—the ghost! In just a few minutes, I hightailed it out of there. Because of all the adrenaline that must have been coursing through my body, I got on the trail, and walked at an excelerated pace that bordered on a run. Soon I met up with two women hikers from Germany who were headed down to the valley floor. Although I'm sure they must have noticed the tormented look on my face, they said nothing. I attempted to act as normal as possible. I told them where I had camped the previous

"I noticed a gathering of people by the side of the bridge who were all wearing blue caps and shorts."

night, and they said they had seen my tent pitched in the meadow. They were pleasant, and soon invited me to accompany them back down the mountain. Not wanting to alarm them, I didn't dare tell them about the ghost I had seen. The three of us made camp that night, without any strange incidents, then we all got up early the next morning, had our breakfast, and were soon back on the trail. After reaching Yosemite Valley at around 1 p.m., we went our separate ways. I was so grateful to be among familiar surroundings, as well as being both mentally and physically exhausted.

As I crossed the last stone bridge that led to my residence, I noticed a gathering of people by the side of the bridge who were all wearing blue caps and shorts. They were holding candles and praying. An uneasiness came over me. I recognized the outfits as the same one the ghost had been wearing. I asked one gentleman what the gathering was for. He said that a friend in their group called "Russell" had died just two days before while swimming in the river. The gathering was to offer prayers to this person before they all got into their cars on their return trip home. After he had finished his sentence, I turned to stone.

With emotion in my voice, I asked him where Russell had died, and how old he was. He told me Russell was 17 years old, and had gone with a group of four on an overnight hiking adventure to Tuolumne Meadows. Apparently, while swimming in one of the deeper streams, he had misjudged a rock's slipperiness, slipped, and fatally struck his head on a rock. I didn't ask any more questions. I walked a few feet away from the gathering, and I began silently, and privately, to sob. I couldn't bring myself to tell him that I had seen the ghost of his friend. I was shaking all over. I watched as the group got into their cars and drove off.

I was a basket case. I felt numb and unable to do much more than think over and over what I had experienced. Thinking took over the remainder of that day, and the next. My thoughts were of life, death, and the unanswered questions I had about the afterlife. I knew I had seen Russell's ghost. The water and blood drops, the cap and shorts, and the manner in which he disappeared on the trail, was all the evidence and proof I would ever need. I had seen a ghost!

"He had misjudged a rocks' slipperiness, slipped, and, fatally struck his head on a rock."

My experience with Russell's ghost took place only four years ago. Since then I've told only a few trusted people. I've discovered that whenever I tell my story to someone, it motivates them to share a story of a ghost experience at the park of their own. Although my personal experience is a hard one to top, fellow Yosemite park employees have some stories that are real chillers.

These days, I don't go hiking alone in the woods without a partner. I'm not necessarily afraid of encountering bears or snakes. It's the "other" type of encounters that I don't ever want to have again. I think you can understand why.

KIMBERLY H. CUNNINGHAM-SUMMERFIELD'S STORY

My foster parents are from the Tuolomne Rancheria. My birth family is from Yukia, California. I am by birth "Tsa'lagi" or Cherokee, but I was raised by my foster parents, in the knowledge and ways of the Yosemite Miwok. I began working at the park at the age of 15, as an Native American Cultural Demonstrator. Today my title is Park Ranger/Interpreter, and I'm also a member of the Park's Native American Cultural staff.

The Native American museum is housed in a park building that was dedicated in 1926, and is constructed of local stone granite. At one corner of the building is an Native American burial whose location is kept secret from the public.

"I began working at the park at the age of 15, as an Native American Cultural Demonstrator."

We don't give out information as to the location of the burial. We respectfully keep that information to ourselves.

I know of many spiritual experiences in the park, Yosemite is full of spirits. And as native people, we believe in the existence of both human and animal spirits. They dwell within the valley's mountains, streams, and waterfalls. They can be seen, and heard moving about, and at times even singing. We believe this. Personally, I'm always experiencing spirits at the park. Right here in the museum, there are many spirits who regularly pay their visits.

Just last week, my two co-workers and I were in the process of closing the museum for the day. We turned off the lights and turned on the alarm system. Finally, standing at the entrance, before locking the doors, we took one last look at the interior, and left. The next morning I came to work at 7:30. As soon as I stepped inside the museum, I "felt" that things weren't right. It was a feeling that just came over me, the feeling that something was out of balance. People say that when a spirit is present, the room will get cold. Maybe that does happen, but I've only experienced the room changing to a very warm temperature when something of a spiritual nature is about to take place.

Suddenly, the lights that are located in the middle of the museum (the ones that specifically spotlight the collection of ceremo-

"Many spirits regularly visit us, right here in the museum"

nial regalia), began to flicker. They'd dim, then slowly get bright, and flicker. It appeared as if someone were playing with them, or sending out a "light code." I explained to my co-worker, "I don't know what's going on, but I'm not going in there!" No one has ever fully explained to me why the lights that focus only on the ceremonial displays behave the way they do sometimes.

All I can say about this is that I know there are spirits in the museum. I've seen them as they walk by, and approach, the area where I am standing. Shadows of people will move about the museum. I've gotten so used to seeing them that I even talk to them. I know that they're always around. Artifacts that are kept under glass, in display cases, occasionally get moved around. I imagine that the creators of these beautiful baskets and such are still emotionally attached to them. It's understandable,

"It appeared as if someone were playing with the lights, or sending out a 'light code'."

because of the love, care, and the creative energy these people have put into their work.

We have one park ranger who we confided in about the spirits in the museum. He made no qualms about his disbelief in the supernatural. But, one evening, as he was closing the museum for the day, something happened to abruptly change his mind. He said that as he was doing a walk through of the museum, not only did he hear voices, but he actually saw the spirits! Since that evening, he's not been the same.

Again, I believe that the artifacts we have in the museum were very personal to the people who skillfully, and lovingly, made them. I've never gotten the feeling that the spirits are angry, just that they are checking up

"Not only did he hear the spirit voices, but he actually saw them!"

on things. The museum does not display anything that is disrespectful to Native American people. The park staff places much importance on not displaying burial jewelry or offerings.

I need to tell you about the mannequins in the museum. The diorama display is actually molded from Native Americans' faces, cast from living people's faces. They'll be times when I'll hear loud shrieks being yelled out by visitors who swear that they've seen the mannequin's heads turn to look at them! I've even had visitors become so scared by the mannequins that they will quickly leave the museum without speaking a word. But I know what took place. Visitors have reported to me that they've seen the eyes, or mouths, move on these mannequins.

My aunts always cautioned me as a child never to look, or stare, at a

"Visitors have reported to me that they've seen the eyes, or mouths, move."

"Their faces were casts from living people's faces."

spirit straight on, because that can cause the spirit harm. I was told that if spirits choose to appear to us, it's because they have a lesson, or news, to give. I was also taught never to be mean, disrespectful, or talk rude about spirits. This is something I have taught my own children. The dead must be respected.

"I've made bows, arrows, nets, string, and other plant-fiber crafts."

RANGER ROBERT L. FRY'S STORY

My position at the park is that of Ranger Naturalist/Interpreter. I'm by profession an ethnobiologist, with a focus in the Native American use of plants. I've made bows, arrows, nets, string, and other plant-fiber crafts. Some of my work is displayed in the museum. This year marks my 42nd year at the park; 13 years as a full-time employee. I came to Yosemite in 1960. Before being employed at the park, I was a high school science teacher. Most of the Native people whom I've talked to privately have described seeing and hearing very unusual things. Without a doubt in their minds, they sincerely believe that spiritual beings do exist at the park.

A common belief is that the dead ancestors return to earth, and to Yosemite, in the physical form of a bear. Because bears have a heel with five toes facing front, a bear's footprint resembles a human's. When Miwoks happen to encounter a bear, they have been taught to look directly at its eyes, and to speak to it normally, just as they would speak to another person. The Miwok never kill bears, believing them to be sacred, or spiritually, pure. A Miwok female friend once described to me that not long after the well-known chief Lamee died in 1955, a bear began to visit her house and the houses of other Native American women's homes in the area. The bear would wonder around the houses and scratch at their windows. During his life the chief, who had never married, was very fond of provoking laughter, and carrying out good-natured pranks on the women. My friend believed that the chief had visited her, and the other women, in the form of this bear. She said they were all a bit unnerved by his visits. I'm also aware that culturally, the Miwok

"Pohono" or Bridalveil Falls.

have a great reverence for, and sometimes fear of, waterfalls. To the Miwok, all waterfalls hold great power, and can prove dangerous if not honored correctly.

Children were never allowed to play or act disrespectfully when in the area of a waterfall. Pohono, or Bridalveil Falls, is a waterfall which is considered to be "haunted" by the Miwok. I personally think it is a very spooky place. The Miwok's name for the Falls, "Pohono," means "bad puffing wind." Pohono is, in my opinion, one of the most beautiful waterfalls in the park. It's 620 feet high, and unlike the other falls in the park, it never ceases to have water spilling over its rim. A common ritual when passing Pohono is to lower one's voice, or cease to speak, until one is quite a distance away. Native Americans believe that spirits dwell at the base of the Pohono, and that these spirits should not be disturbed.

The famous collector, Ripley, once labeled Pohono, "The

waterfall that flows uphill." He coined this phrase because, at times, usually in the month of September, there is a peculiar wind that hits the face of the waterfall with such force, that if the flow of water is low enough, it will push the water back, and cause it to stop flowing for a few seconds. Soon after, a huge amount of this restricted water will spill over the side in a gush.

I had an unusual experience with Pohono, which took place at 2 a.m. At the time, I was headed to a favorite fishing spot. The weather was calm, but as soon as I entered the area of the Falls, I noticed that, strangely, the trees were whipping wildly back and forth. Knowing what I did about the spiritual identity of the Falls, I felt the strong urge to get out of my car, which I did, and said, "Oh, Pohono I honor you." Feeling personally convinced that I had done the right thing, I drove away.

Another strange thing associated with Pohono was described to me in 1973 by Dave Jarel, the Head of the Park's Heli-Attack crew. There had been a very heavy winter, which had dropped a lot of snow on the park. Badger Pass ski area, which is located about five miles back from the Fall's rim, is used by many skiers to reach Dewie Point. There had been two skiers, a doctor and his son, who had decided to use this route. They had become lost in a snowstorm and the son had decided to turn back, but the father had chosen to continue. The father had become lost and somehow had ended up at the lip of Bridalveil Falls. Obviously, there was no way down. Unable to locate him, his body had not been discovered until the early spring thaw. Dave said that as he was making a pass over the falls in his helicopter, he had noticed a red patch of cloth at the rim. He had swung the helicopter around for a closer look, and had recognized it to be the lost skier. As the ground crew approached the body, they had noticed he had been frozen in a sitting position on a rock, with his chin in his hand, blankly starring at the valley below. His skis had been eventually located wedged among the boulders down below, at the Fall's base. He had apparently taken them off in frustration, and had tossed them over the side. I say frustration, because the road down below is open year-round, and he must have died watching the cars pass below, knowing that the drivers were unaware of his grave situation up above. One year, the skull of a young girl was found at Summit Meadow, again in the Badger Pass area. Many years after this girl had been murdered in the park, the murderer was arrested in Texas on another charge. I guess his conscience got the better of him, because he had described in grim detail to the authorities where and how he had committed the murder in Yosemite. I happened to be with the medical forensic examiner from Seattle, who was examining the

Above Bridalveil Falls is the upper valley of Bridalveil Creek. The creek once flowed down an incline to join the Merced River. Ice Age glaciers filled and widened the main canyon, sheered its granite walls, and bulldozed away the lower stream channel. When the ice melted, Bridalveil Creek was left hanging—with a 620-foot drop to the river. Around the Valley are similar glacier-chopped side streams such as Yosemite, Ribbon, and Sentinel Falls.

skull's teeth. We had searched for bones, and other evidence, but all we had located was the skull. The examiner explained how animals will usually drag away most of the body's bones, except for the skull. Due to its round shape, the skull is difficult for animals to bite, or grasp a hold of. The skull is usually the only portion of the body that is left at the murder site.

I also know of a man who had committed a gruesome suicide in 1958 by jumping off Half Dome. He had been staying at the Glacier Point Hotel, which in 1969 was consumed, and destroyed, by a massive fire. He had left a note in his room stating, among other things, that he was going to hike the nine miles to Half Dome. Another note had been found where he had jumped. It had been folded in his coat pocket and had stated his intentions. At the base of the rock the search party had located most of his body, everything but one leg. Glacier Point also has been the site of a suicide/homicide. A disgruntled man had apparently pushed the woman he had been with over the edge, then he followed her by jumping to his death. Another sad case I'm aware of is that of an obese, 350-pound man who had committed suicide by jumping to his death off Taft Point. Taft Point is just west of Glacier Point. This man also happened to be an employee of the Park.

I know that each of us experience paranormal events in our own, personal way. And, I also think the human mind is flexible enough to believe whatever it wants. I believe, and "feel" a parallel "connection" to native people, and to the men from ancient times who fashioned arrowheads. These people didn't have much control over nature, and when you have very little

An example of Ranger Fry's excellent craftsmanship.

control, you become very respectful of Nature's power. To the native people of Yosemite, it was a given fact that the spiritual forces of coyote, frog, bear, lizard, to name a few, all had their functions. Overseeing everything was the great Creator who lived beyond the setting sun. When the original inhabitants died, their bodies were cremated, in order to set the spirit free to join the Great One.

CRUZ GARCIA JR.'S STORY

I've been employed at the park for 30 years. I was born and raised in Bakersfield, California, until the age of 22. I attended the University of Fresno State for three years, then made the move to Yosemite. I've been at the Park ever since. Currently my position is Head of Housekeeping. Initially, employees were very open about discussing their personal stories regarding encounters with ghosts at the Park. So many strange things happen at Yosemite, I'm personally surprised that more of the public isn't aware of what goes on here. Of

"Leydig Meadow has been the site for many strange occurrences."

course, some are simply rumors, but many of these "so-called" rumors have been confirmed by the park rangers. I myself have confirmed some of these stories by tracking down older employees who had worked here before I was employed at the Park. I personally have experienced spiritual manifestations, or ghosts. Because of my own family, and cultural upbringing, I am aware that these things do exist. As I said, Yosemite is filled with ghosts, and spots of spiritual power. Unfortunate as it is, Yosemite has also experienced many deadly events. People have chosen to commit suicide by jumping off the falls, and there have even been several documented murders. And then there are the numerous accidental deaths, from falls and drownings. From day one, I was told about the different public buildings, and certain meadows, that were known to be haunted. Leydig Meadow is one of the better known.

Leydig Meadow is located directly behind our Housekeeping office, and has been the location for many strange occurrences. I've known of weird incidents where employees who have been "drawn" to sleep out in Leydig Meadow, and the next day at work, when fellow employees have noticed that the employee is missing, have searched the meadow, and not found the individual. Later in the day, when the "missing" person was spotted at his job, surprised friends have asked for an explanation. The employee would answer that he, or she, was unaware of any search party. Apparently, the meadow offers a sort of power to disguise, or hide, people. I know that the persons it envelopes is unable to see, or even hear, the cries of others that are searching for them. It's a sort of "mesmerizing" of the senses that takes over the body. I've now heard of the meadow referred to as a "power source." People have also told me that they've even seen people or "spirits" positioned in the tree branches that have grown in the meadow. No one is absolutely sure why, or how, this power source came to be. I've been told that the National Park Service has records of strange occurrences taking place in the meadow, which go back for many years, but they've never been willing to disclose this information. It's difficult to personally research this, unless you are able to get the cooperation of the Park Service.

As the Head of Housekeeping for the Yosemite Lodge, members of

"Members of my staff have approached me several times, to tell me about different incidents where they have seen faces reflected in the mirrors of certain rooms."

my staff have approached me several times to tell me about different incidents where they have seen faces reflected in the mirrors of certain rooms, and lights that strangely have begun to dim in rooms when someone has entered. Mirrors have also disappeared from walls, and have later been found in unusual places, or tightly forced into drawers, to the point of becoming stuck.

Maids have witnessed numerous incidences. Upon entering rooms with unmade beds, they've turned their attention away for a few seconds, then turned around again, and the bed has been made! They've also seen the indentations of an invisible

body lying on the mattress of a freshly made bed. I've personally been witness to several of these occurrences at the lodge. I had a maid so disturbed by the spirits that she refused to clean one particular room, unless another maid was with her.

Maids' cleaning supplies, bottles, brushes, and so forth have been moved, and placed in areas where they shouldn't have been. Further common experiences have been doors that are opened or closed without a person present. Maids have nervously reported being watched by an unseen presence, that follows them from room to room. I remember a maid who had reported that three of her heavy linen bags that she had filled with soiled sheets, towels, etcetera, were mysteriously removed from the first floor where she was working. She was alone at the time, and was unnerved when she discovered the bags mysteriously had been moved to the bottom floor of the lodge. The bags could only have been moved by someone passing by her, but she had not seen anyone physically move them. One maid was so frightened by what had happened to her in one room, that her only means of escape had been to dash to the balcony and climb on to the roof on the second floor! I remember when she did this, and the ladders that were brought to the lodge. Eventually she was coaxed down. Following the incident, she was so terrified by what had happened to her in that room, she quite her job!

All these strange things took place in the older portion of the lodge, which had been damaged, then had been permanently dismantled and removed in the immense Yosemite flood of 1997. The original lodge had consisted of 16 rooms, and above them had been the attic, which had been built sometime in the early 1950s. One original staff member employed at the lodge was a woman named Mildred. This information is important to the hauntings, because Mildred worked primarily in the original building as a maid. As I said, the original portion of the lodge is where all the spiritual occurrences were reported to have taken place.

This is how the story was told to me. One day, Mildred had been reported missing. After a search had been initiated, her lifeless body had been eventually located hanging from a rope that was attached to one of the rafters in the lodge's attic. The attic had been built in such a manner so as to connect the two original lodge buildings. Now, here is where the story gets interesting. It had been reported that Mildred had committed suicide, but a witness at the scene had later stated that her hands had been bound with a cord. So was it suicide or a murder? Not long after, a curious employee had come forward to say that she was so intrigued to see the attic where Mildred had been found hanging that she had taken it upon herself to "borrow" the key to the attic's door and view the area for herself. She told me that she had happened to notice several mirrors that had been lying against a wall. She had glanced at one of the mirrors, and suddenly had seen a woman's face staring back at her! She had described the woman as being middle-aged, and with somewhat grayish hair.

Because of her fright, that was all the employee had been able to remember before she rapidly had exited the attic. Apparently, when the original lodge had been removed, Mildred had ceased to want to hang around.

I've personally known several of the people that have reported these incidents to me. I knew them well enough to be able to say that they were credible and sincere. I could see that they were visibly shaken by what they had experienced. As of today, I haven't heard of any further hauntings at the lodge.

Yosemite has attracted numerous types of individuals who have even attempted to misuse its spiritual areas for their own personal gain. I was aware of several staff members, who had been employed several years ago at the Park, that were involved in Satan worship. Employees reported seeing one of these employee's rooms filled with lit, black candles and upturned crucifixes. On one wall of his room he even had the Lord's Prayer written backwards, which he had hung on his wall.

I want to make clear the distinction between witchcraft and Satanism. Witchcraft, or "Wicca," is historically a beneficial religion that a person or community, benefits from. It's an Earth-based religion. However, the worship of Satanism is totally different from that which practicing Wiccans believe in. Most people confuse Wicca with Satanism—they are not the same. This guy with the candles was a Satanist. He made no claims to hide this fact. He was also heavily into drugs. Eventually, he was fired. But what amazed me was why he hadn't been fired sooner. Again, this all took place many years ago.

Throughout the years, there have been other incidences of "spiritual" power trips that I've heard of. I still hear the stories of people going to Yosemite's meadows and trails attempting to contact spirits, with Ouija boards, and fortune-telling devices. I  think these people are not capable of handling what the natural forces have to offer. I think they should leave the spirits, and power sources, alone. The spirits have always been "free floating" at the Park. They should be left alone.

The End

FINIS CORONAT

References

California State Parks Magazine, 2001 Tenth Edition, Meredith Corporation.

"A Professional Guide," California Native American Heritage Commission.

"History of Tuolumne County," by Sandy Esau and Patricia Newton, Tuolumne County Visitors Bureau.

"History of Sutter Creek," Sutter Creek Visitors Center.

"History of Nevada City," Nevada City Chamber of Commerce

"The Miwok In Yosemite," Yosemite Association.

The Old Sacramento News, Published by Capitol Weekly Corporation

History of the Groveland Hotel," by Peggy A. Mosley. "

"History of the National Hotel," by Stephen Willey.

"Mannequin of Mr. Twain," Mark Twain Bookstore, Virginia City, Nevada.

"Baskets by Selena La Mare" and "Atsugewi," Lassen Loomis Museum Assoc.

"Encounters with Death—History of Azrael," by Leilah Wendell.

Chambers of Commerce and Points of Interest in the Gold Rush Country

Calaveras Visitors Bureau (800) 225-3764

Marshall Gold Discovery State Park (916) 622-3470

The Groveland Hotel (800) 273-3314

Lassen County Chamber of Commerce (530) 257-4323

The National Hotel (800) 894-3446

Shasta Historical Society (530) 243-3720

City of Oroville (530-538-2401

Amador Chamber of Commerce (800) 649-4988

Tuolunme County Visitors Bureau (800) 446-1333

Golden Flower Trading Company & Museum (530) 265-6686

Murphys Historic Hotel & Lodge (800) 532-7684

Passages Home Accessories (209) 267-5225

Hangman's Tree Bar (530) 622-3878

Sacramento Historic Sites Assn. (916) 442-4966

Aaron Brothers Art & Framing (530) 223-0992

Wild Rose & Mary (209) 728-9453

Nevada City Chamber of Commerce (530) 265-2692

Sutter Creek Visitors Center (209) 267-1344

Sutter's Fort State Park (916) 445-4422

California State Indian Museum (916) 324-0971

Gold Bug Mine & Park (530) 642-5232

Mercer Caverns (209) 728-2101

Caverns of California (888) 818-7462

Yosemite Sierra Visitors Bureau (559) 683-4636

Coulterville Visitor Center (209) 878-3074

Mariposa County Visitor Bureau (800) 208-2434

Yosemite Association (209) 379-2646

Sutter Gold Mine (888) 818-7462

Redding Convention & Visitors Bureau (800) 874-7562

Columbia Chamber of Commerce (209)536-1672

Nevada City's Chinese Quarter Society (530) 265-0577

Yosemite National Park (209) 372-0200

Other Books
by Antonio R. Garcez

American Indian Ghost Stories
of the Southwest
ISBN 0-9634029-7-8

Ghost Stories of Arizona
Originally published as
Adobe Angels—Ghost Stories of Arizona
ISBN 0-9740988-0-9

Ghost Stories of New Mexico
Originally published as
The Adobe Angels New Mexico series
ISBN 0-9634029-9-4

Future books will include research, and travels into,
other states of the Union, covering the fascinating
subject of the human psyche. As always, you are
all welcome to come along for the ride.

About the Author

Antonio R. Garcez graduated with a B. A. degree from California State University at Northridge, then attended Graduate school at the University of Wisconsin. Antonio resides, and continues to write from, his home in New Mexico.